T0205837

Communications
in Computer and Information Science 1922

Rationale

The CCIS series is devoted to the publication of proceedings of computer science conferences. Its aim is to efficiently disseminate original research results in informatics in printed and electronic form. While the focus is on publication of peer-reviewed full papers presenting mature work, inclusion of reviewed short papers reporting on work in progress is welcome, too. Besides globally relevant meetings with internationally representative program committees guaranteeing a strict peer-reviewing and paper selection process, conferences run by societies or of high regional or national relevance are also considered for publication.

Topics

The topical scope of CCIS spans the entire spectrum of informatics ranging from foundational topics in the theory of computing to information and communications science and technology and a broad variety of interdisciplinary application fields.

Information for Volume Editors and Authors

Publication in CCIS is free of charge. No royalties are paid, however, we offer registered conference participants temporary free access to the online version of the conference proceedings on SpringerLink (http://link.springer.com) by means of an http referrer from the conference website and/or a number of complimentary printed copies, as specified in the official acceptance email of the event.

CCIS proceedings can be published in time for distribution at conferences or as post-proceedings, and delivered in the form of printed books and/or electronically as USBs and/or e-content licenses for accessing proceedings at SpringerLink. Furthermore, CCIS proceedings are included in the CCIS electronic book series hosted in the SpringerLink digital library at http://link.springer.com/bookseries/7899. Conferences publishing in CCIS are allowed to use Online Conference Service (OCS) for managing the whole proceedings lifecycle (from submission and reviewing to preparing for publication) free of charge.

Publication process

The language of publication is exclusively English. Authors publishing in CCIS have to sign the Springer CCIS copyright transfer form, however, they are free to use their material published in CCIS for substantially changed, more elaborate subsequent publications elsewhere. For the preparation of the camera-ready papers/files, authors have to strictly adhere to the Springer CCIS Authors' Instructions and are strongly encouraged to use the CCIS LaTeX style files or templates.

Abstracting/Indexing

CCIS is abstracted/indexed in DBLP, Google Scholar, EI-Compendex, Mathematical Reviews, SCImago, Scopus. CCIS volumes are also submitted for the inclusion in ISI Proceedings.

How to start

To start the evaluation of your proposal for inclusion in the CCIS series, please send an e-mail to ccis@springer.com.

Yang Feng · Chong Feng
Editors

Machine Translation

19th China Conference, CCMT 2023
Jinan, China, October 19–21, 2023
Proceedings

 Springer

Editors
Yang Feng
Institute of Computing Technology Chinese
Academy of Sciences
Beijing, China

Chong Feng
Beijing Institute of Technology
Beijing, China

ISSN 1865-0929   ISSN 1865-0937 (electronic)
Communications in Computer and Information Science
ISBN 978-981-99-7893-9   ISBN 978-981-99-7894-6 (eBook)
https://doi.org/10.1007/978-981-99-7894-6

This Springer imprint is published by the registered company Springer Nature Singapore Pte Ltd.
The registered company address is: 152 Beach Road, #21-01/04 Gateway East, Singapore 189721, Singapore

Paper in this product is recyclable.

Preface

The China Conference on Machine Translation (CCMT) is a national annual academic conference held by the Machine Translation Committee of the Chinese Information Processing Society of China (CIPS) which brings together researchers and practitioners in the area of machine translation, providing a forum for those in academia and industry to exchange and promote the latest developments in methodologies, resources, projects, and products, with a special emphasis on the languages in China. Since the first session of CCMT in 2005, 18 sessions have been successfully organized (the previous 14 sessions were called CWMT), and a total of 12 machine translation evaluations (2007, 2008, 2009, 2011, 2013, 2015, 2017, 2018, 2019, 2020, 2021, 2022) have been organized, as well as one open-source system module development (2006) and two strategic seminars (2010, 2012). These activities have made a substantial impact on advancing the research and development of machine translation in China. The conference has been a highly productive forum for the progress of this area and is considered a leading and important academic event in the natural language processing field in China.

This year, the 19th CCMT took place in Jinan, Shandong. This conference continued the tradition of being the most important academic event dedicated to advancing machine translation research in China. It hosted the 13th Machine Translation Evaluation Campaign, featured two keynote speeches, and included two tutorials. The conference also organized five panel discussions, bringing attention to multimodal machine translation, large language models for machine translation, the industry of machine translation, the frontier of machine translation, and the forum for PhD students. A total of 71 submissions (including 27 English papers and 44 Chinese papers) were received for the conference. All papers were carefully reviewed in a double-blind manner and each paper was evaluated by at least three members of an international Program Committee. From the submissions, 11 English papers and 20 Chinese papers were accepted. These papers address all aspects of machine translation, including improvement of translation models and systems, translation quality estimation, document-level machine translation, low-resource machine translation, etc. We would like to express our thanks to every person and institution involved in the organization of this conference, especially the Program Committee, the machine translation evaluation campaign, the invited speakers, the local organization team, the generous sponsors, and the organizations that supported and promoted the event. Last but not least, we greatly appreciate Springer for publishing the proceedings.

October 2023

Yang Feng
Chong Feng

Organization

General Chairs

Min Zhang — Harbin Institute of Technology at Shenzhen, China

Yinglong Wang — Qilu University of Technology, China

General Vice-chairs

Meihong Yang — Qilu University of Technology, China

Minglei Shu — Qilu University of Technology, China

Xiaoming Wu — Qilu University of Technology, China

Program Committee Co-chairs

Yang Feng — ICT, Chinese Academy of Sciences, China

Chong Feng — Beijing Institute of Technology, China

Evaluation Chairs

Yating Yang — Xinjiang Technical Institute of Physics and Chemistry, Chinese Academy of Sciences, China

Rui Wang — Shanghai Jiao Tong University, China

Organizing Co-chairs

Jiajun Zhang — Institute of Automation, Chinese Academy of Sciences, China

Wenpeng Lu — Qilu University of Technology, China

Special Forum Co-chairs

Xing Wang   Tencent AI Lab, China
Kehai Chen   Harbin Institute of Technology at Shenzhen,
                             China

Tutorial Co-chairs

Peng Li   Tsinghua University, China
Liangyou Li   Huawei, China

Student Forum Co-chairs

Hao Zhou   Tsinghua University, China
Jingjing Xu   Shanghai Artificial Intelligence Research
                             Institute, China

Front-Trends Forum Co-chairs

Mingxuan Wang   ByteDance, China
Yang Zhao   Chinese Academy of Sciences, China

Co-chairs of Industrial Application Forum

Jingbo Zhu   Northeastern University, China
Guoping Huang   Tencent AI Lab, China

Publication Co-chairs

Shengxiang Gao   Kunming University of Science and Technology,
                             China
Yachao Li   Northwest Minzu University, China

Sponsorship Co-chairs

Yidong Chen	Xiamen University, China
Shujian Huang	Nanjing University, China

Publicity Co-chairs

Junhui Li	Soochow University, China
Hao Yang	Huawei, China
Weiyu Zhang	Qilu University of Technology, China
Chaoqun Zheng	Qilu University of Technology, China

Program Committee

Baosong Yang	Alibaba Group, China
Biao Zhang	University of Edinburgh, UK
Bojie Hu	Tencent, China
Changxing Wu	East China Jiaotong University, China
Chong Feng	Beijing Institute of Technology, China
Chunliang Zhang	Northeastern University, China
Cunli Mao	Kunming University of Science and Technology, China
Dakun Zhang	Systran, France
Derek F. Wong	University of Macau, China
Fandong Meng	Tencent, China
Guoping Huang	Tencent AI Lab, China
Hailong Cao	Harbin Institute of Technology, China
Haitao Mi	Tencent America, USA
Heng Yu	Shopee, China
Hongfei Xu	Zhengzhou University, China
Jiajun Zhang	Institute of Automation, Chinese Academy of Sciences, China
Jinan Xu	Beijing Jiaotong University, China
Jinhua Du	Xi'an University of Technology, China
Jinsong Su	Xiamen University, China
Juan Pino	Meta Fundamental AI Research, USA
Jun Xie	Alibaba DAMO Academy, China
Junhui Li	Soochow University, China
Junliang Guo	Microsoft Research Asia, China
Kehai Chen	Harbin Institute of Technology (Shenzhen), China

Lemao Liu	Tencent AI Lab, China
Liangyou Li	Huawei Noah's Ark Lab, China
Longyue Wang	Tencent AI Lab, China
Maoxi Li	Jiangxi Normal University, China
Mingxuan Wang	Bytedance AI Lab, China
Muhua Zhu	Meituan Group, China
Muyun Yang	Harbin Institute of Technology, China
Qiang Wang	Hithink RoyalFlush AI Research Institute, China
Quan Du	NiuTrans, China
Qun Liu	Huawei Noah's Ark Lab, China
Shengxiang Gao	Kunming University of Science and Technology, China
Shuangzhi Wu	Bytedance, China
Shujian Huang	Nanjing University, China
Tong Xiao	Northeastern University, China
Toshiaki Nakazawa	University of Tokyo, Japan
Wen Zhang	Xiaomi AI Lab, China
Xiang Li	Xiaomi AI Lab, China
Xiangyu Duan	Soochow University, China
Xiaocheng Feng	Harbin Institute of Technology, China
Xiaofeng Wu	Apple, Ireland
Xing Wang	Tencent AI Lab, China
Xu Tan	Microsoft Research Asia, China
Yachao Li	Northwest Minzu University, China
Yang Feng	ICT, Chinese Academy of Sciences, China
Yang Liu	Tsinghua University, China
Yidong Chen	Xiamen University, China
Yufeng Chen	Beijing Jiaotong University, China
Yves Lepage	Waseda University, Japan
Zhaopeng Tu	Tencent AI Lab, China
Zhengxian Gong	Soochow University, China

Organizer

Chinese Information Processing Society of China, China

Qilu University of Technology, China

Sponsors

Diamond Sponsor

Global Tone Communication Technology Co., Ltd.

Platinum Sponsors

NiuTrans Research

Youdao

HUAWEI Translate

Cloud Translation

Gold Sponsors

OPPO Corporation

Baidu

Xiaomi Corporation

Silver Sponsor

NEWTRANX Technology

Contents

Transn's Submission for CCMT 2023 Quality Estimation Task

Zeyu Yan[✉], Wenbo Zhang, Qiaobo Deng, Hongbao Mao, Jie Cai, and Zhengyu He

Transn IOL Technology Co., Ltd., Wuhan 430070, Hubei, China
yzyalbert@gmail.com

Abstract. Machine translation quality estimation is a kind of technique to rate and choose the best translation from several translations of text in source language, which is suitable for the application trend of machine translation in international communication. CCMT 2023 Quality Estimate Task focuses on predicting sentence level score for each sentence pair in English to/from Chinese. This paper describes our methods for predicting Human Translation Edit Rate (HTER) score of sentence pairs in both directions. Various source-translation interactive structures are explored to enhance the representations of source and translation to make a more accurate prediction. On account of the well-known powerful ability of pretrained language models, the combinations between varied pretrained language models and interactive structures are also searched to obtain better model performance. Meanwhile, some pretraining methods and the ensemble method are applied to boost the single model performance on Dev and Test data. Our method gets competitive results in both directions with these augmentations.

Keywords: Quality Estimation · Pretrained Language Model · Text Matching

1 Introduction

Machine translation has been widely used nowadays, which requires a quality estimation system to ensure its appropriate usage. However, traditional estimation methods depend on pure human judgment, which is inefficient and resource-intensive. It is important to accomplish automatic translation quality estimation with high efficiency and low cost. Machine translation Quality Estimation (QE) is an automatic evaluation method for choosing the best translation from several machine-translated sentences (*mt*) candidates of one source sentence (*src*) without reference (*ref*).

QE can be realized at sentence level or word level. Sentence level QE aims at predicting a quality score of *mt* sentence and word level QE aims at predicting an OK/BAD label for each word in *mt* to indicate whether this word is translated properly or improperly. The quality estimation task of CCMT 2023 focuses on

English to/from Chinese language directions and predicts Human Translation Edit Rate (HTER) [7,16] score for each *mt* sentence, where HTER measures the number of editing that needs to perform to change *mt* into *ref*. Our method utilizes different pretrained language models (PLMs) to encode sentence pairs and predict HTER score. We also explore new pretraining approaches for quality estimation and the deep interaction between words in *src* and *mt*, which shows significant improvements on this task. In addition, ensemble methods boost model performance not surprisingly.

2   Related Work

Quality Estimation algorithms before deep learning usually extract various features from word, POS tags, syntax, length, and other binary features presenting different aspects in *src* or *mt*. Then a machine learning model uses these features to make predictions. Many machine learning tools are designed for this purpose like QuEst [1] and QuEst++ [2]. Such procedures can be abstracted as the predictor-estimator framework [11].

After the broad usage of neural networks and Transformers [10], deep learning models play the role of feature extractor or even score estimator. DeepQuest [3] and OpenKiwi [4] provide tools for multilevel quality estimation by adopting neural networks. In recent years, TransQuest [5] and COMET [6] have shown significant improvements in quality estimation tasks, by using big PLM as feature extractor and then predicting sentence-level scores or word-level labels. These models encode *src* and its *mt* into high dimensional embedding vectors through multilingual PLMs, then input another neural network to get quality predictions. Diverse multilingual PLMs can perform as sentence encoder such as mBERT [8], XLM-RoBERTa [21], InfoXLM [20], mDeBERTa [19], RemBERT [22] and so on.

3   Feature-Enhanced Estimator for Sentence-Level QE

3.1   Model Architecture

Quality estimation task involves measuring the editing number in *mt* word by word, which expects the meaning of each word to be translated precisely and unambiguously. PLMs like BERT [8] and RoBERTa [9] have revealed marvelous capability of representation and feature extraction in natural language processing. Consequently, our model designs several feature interactive structures between *src* and *mt* after being encoded by multilingual PLM encoders. Both *src* and *mt* are concatenated and input into PLM to get their last hidden state representations $(s_1, s_2, ..., s_m)$ and $(t_1, t_2, ..., t_n)$, where m and n are word numbers of *src* and *mt* as shown in Eq. 1 and Eq. 2. Afterward, three kinds of feature interactive modules are completed on top of PLMs as illustrated in Fig. 1.

$$outputs = PLM\_encoder([src; mt]) \tag{1}$$

$$[s_1, s_2, ..., s_m], [t_1, t_2, ..., t_n] = split\_src\_mt(outputs) \tag{2}$$

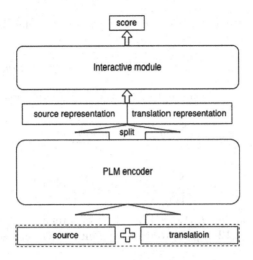

Fig. 1. Model architecture with interactive module

Simple Interactive Module (SIM). Following the settings of CometKiwi [12], we use the mean pooling to generate the vector representations of *src* and *mt*. Then the element-wise product and subtraction results between *src* and *mt* representations are concatenated together with the vector representations of *src* and *mt*. A MLP module predicts HTER score based on these representations as follows:

$$s_{mean} = mean\_pooling([s_1, s_2, ..., s_m]) \tag{3}$$

$$t_{mean} = mean\_pooling([t_1, t_2, ..., t_m]) \tag{4}$$

$$hter = MLP([s_{mean}; t_{mean}; s_{mean} \odot t_{mean}; |s_{mean} - t_{mean}|]) \tag{5}$$

RNN-Based Interactive Module (RIM). Recurrent neural network (RNN) is a popular model in the natural language processing area, which can capture intra-sentence dependency in a text sequence. Therefore, we use the Bidirectional LSTM [15] (BiLSTM) layer to encode the word-level output hidden states of the encoders for further reinforcing the feature interactions and predicting HTER scores between *src* and *mt* as follows:

$$lstm\_output = BiLSTM([s_1, s_2, ..., s_m; t_1, t_2, ..., t_m]) \tag{6}$$

$$hter = MLP(mean\_pooling(lstm\_output)) \tag{7}$$

Multilevel Interactive Module (MIM). Inspired by ESIM [14] and RE2 [13], the cross attention between *src* and *mt* reflects the similarity between words in different languages. Considering that different layers in an encoder catch different levels of information of *src* and *mt*, we determine to combine these two kinds of features to strengthen the representations of *src* and *mt*. Specifically, a weighted sum of layer-wise hidden states of *src* or *mt*

$$s^l = mean\_pooling([s_1^l, s_2^l, ..., s_m^l]), for\,each\,layer\,l \tag{8}$$

$$t^l = mean\_pooling([t_1^l, t_2^l, ..., t_n^l]), for\,each\,layer\,l \tag{9}$$

$$s_{mix} = \sum_{l=1}^{L} w_s^l \cdot s^l, where \sum_{l=1}^{L} w_s^l = 1 \tag{10}$$

$$t_{mix} = \sum_{l=1}^{L} w_t^l \cdot t^l, where \sum_{l=1}^{L} w_t^l = 1 \tag{11}$$

with a total layer number L (Eq. 8–Eq. 11) is concatenated with its cross attention layer output (Eq. 12–Eq. 16) to transform into a rich representation through MLP layer.

$$e_{ij} = s_i^T t_j \tag{12}$$

$$s_i^{ca} = \sum_{j=1}^{n} \frac{exp(e_{ij})}{\sum_{k=1}^{n} exp(e_{ik})} t_j, \forall i \in [1, 2, ..., m] \tag{13}$$

$$t_j^{ca} = \sum_{i=1}^{m} \frac{exp(e_{ij})}{\sum_{k=1}^{m} exp(e_{kj})} s_i, \forall j \in [1, 2, ..., n] \tag{14}$$

$$s_{ca} = mean\_pooling([s_1^{ca}, s_2^{ca}, ..., s_m^{ca}]) \tag{15}$$

$$t_{ca} = mean\_pooling([t_1^{ca}, t_2^{ca}, ..., t_n^{ca}]) \tag{16}$$

Features of *src* and *mt* are fused separately (Eq. 17, Eq. 18) for further combination.

$$s_{comb} = MLP([s_{ca}; s_{mix}; |s_{ca} \odot s_{mix}|; s_{ca} - s_{mix}]) \tag{17}$$

$$t_{comb} = MLP([t_{ca}; t_{mix}; |t_{ca} \odot t_{mix}|; t_{ca} - t_{mix}]) \tag{18}$$

Then HTER score is computed by another MLP layer.

$$hter = MLP([s_{comb}; t_{comb}]) \tag{19}$$

This module is illustrated in Fig. 3.

Loss Selection. We choose the Mean Squared Error (MSE) loss for finetuning models. Besides, the square root of the original HTER score is set as label when using MSE loss since the distribution of HTER score in training data is dense in lower score range (see Fig. 2).

$$loss = MSE(hter_{pred}, \sqrt{hter_{true}}) \tag{20}$$

Taking the square root of HTER score can increase the divergence among different scores and make model predict easier.

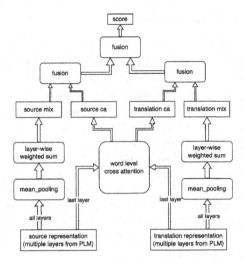

Fig. 2. The ranking of HTER scores on En-Zh training data in ascending order

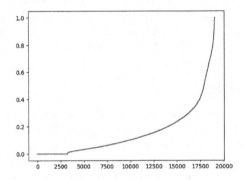

Fig. 3. The structure of Multilevel Interactive Module

3.2   Pretraining Corpus Generation

Transformer models often need plenty of training data for supervised learning so we need to generate more data for pretraining quality estimation models from bilingual parallel corpus. Motivated by [17], to generate *mt* data, we use several open-source neural machine translation models, including mbart50-m2m [28], Helsinki NLP Opus-en-zh [29], Helsinki NLP Opus-zh-en [30], M2M100 [31] and NLLB [32], which are provided by huggingface.com.

Some simple rules like length restriction and removal of special characters together with LaBSE [18] model are used to filter semantically unrelated sentence pairs from the original parallel corpus and we sample part of the filtered parallel corpus due to the computing power limit. For each sentence pair in sampled parallel corpus, we translate both sentences from one language to another, from which we can get two pairs of *src* and *mt*. Then we compute the HTER score between *mt* and *ref* by using sacrebleu [27] and filter out those sentence pairs with HTER score greater than 1.

After these steps, we generate nearly three million of (*src, mt, ref, hter score*) tuples as pretraining dataset before finetuning on the quality estimation dataset. These data are utilized to do two separate pretraining tasks on encoders. The first task *mlm* is mask language modeling on pretraining dataset, identically in BERT-like models [8,9,21]. Both *src* and *ref* are concatenated and masked partial words randomly as input into encoder, and encoder predicts what the masked tokens should be. Another pretraining task *hter* is predicting HTER scores on pretraining dataset based on concatenated *src* and *mt* with MSE loss.

3.3   Model Ensemble

Since several models are finetuned to predict HTER scores, we need to do model filtering and ensemble for better results developed on Dev set. For model filtering, we select the models with a higher Pearson correlation coefficient. Then we integrate the results from different models by two means. The first way is simply averaging models' scores to get the final prediction score for each *mt*

$$score = \frac{1}{model\_num} \sum_{i=1}^{model\_num} score_i \tag{21}$$

and the second method is to calculate the weighted sum of predictions of one sample, where the weights are the performance rank of each model on Dev set for each language pair.

$$total = \sum_{i=1}^{model\_rank} i \tag{22}$$

$$score = \sum_{i=1}^{model\_rank} \frac{i}{total} score_i \tag{23}$$

4   Experiments

4.1   Datasets

We use the data from CCMT 2023 Machine Translation Quality Estimation tasks for model finetuning while restoring the tokenized sentences to the original forms by removing spaces. The bilingual parallel dataset for CCMT 2023 Chinese-English translation task is filtered and used for pretraining as described in Sect. 3.2. The QE dataset statistics are shown in Table 1.

Table 1. QE data statistics of CCMT Quality Estimation Task

language pair	Train	Dev
En-Zh	19060	1528
Zh-En	13983	1412

4.2   Training and Evaluation

Training and model Python codes are completed with PyTorch [24] 1.13 and transformers [25] 4.26.1. All models are trained on NVIDIA GeForce RTX 3090 24G for both pretraining on pretraining corpus and finetuning on quality estimation data. Models are finetuned by AdamW [23] optimizer with learning rate of 1e−5, max sequence length of 128, batch size of 16, and 3 epochs. The model checkpoint with the best Pearson correlation coefficient calculated by SciPy [26] on Dev set is selected for Test set. Chinese-to-English and English-to-Chinese directions are trained and evaluated separately. We also evaluate finetuned results with and without pretraining.

4.3   Results and Analysis

The following Tables 2 and Table 3 show the Pearson correlation coefficient results of different encoders with different interactive modules on Dev set. These models are pretrained on *hter* task at first. When the interactive module fuses more diverse features from encoder, the Pearson correlation coefficient grows even with different encoders with respect to models with encoder only.

However, the pretraining approaches described in Sect. 3.2 have positive or negative effects on different encoders shown in Table 4 when using encoders and multilevel interactive module. The *hter* improves the performance of all models which reveals that the amount of training data is the key to superior quality estimation. The *mlm* boosts the performance of most models except InfoXLM and RemBert. A probable explanation for this is that InfoXLM is pretrained in a contrastive learning way [20] while mask language modeling is harmful to the original capability. And RemBert has a similar reason for this phenomenon [22].

Table 2. Results on En-Zh Dev set of interactive modules in Sect. 3.1

Language pair	En-Zh			
interactive module	no module	SIM	RIM	MIM
XLM-RoBERTa-Large	0.3526	0.3160	0.3315	0.3626
InfoXLM-Large	0.4067	0.4454	0.4588	0.4603
mBERT	0.2633	0.3545	0.3369	0.3345
RemBert	0.3100	0.3632	0.3676	0.3309
mDeBERTa-v3-base	0.3548	0.4002	0.4005	0.4025

Table 3. Results on Zh-En Dev set of interactive modules in Sect. 3.1

Language pair	Zh-En			
interactive module	no module	SIM	RIM	MIM
XLM-RoBERTa-Large	0.4855	0.4462	0.4994	0.4486
InfoXLM-large	0.4641	0.5299	0.5252	0.4763
mBERT	0.4235	0.4505	0.4369	0.4557
RemBert	0.4573	0.5178	0.5193	0.5046
mDeBERTa-v3-base	0.4872	0.4920	0.5064	0.4918

Table 4. Results on Dev set of pretraining methods

Language pair	En-Zh			Zh-En		
pretraining method	mlm	hter	mlm+hter	mlm	hter	mlm+hter
XLM-RoBERTa-Large	0.4147	0.3664	0.4563	0.5199	0.4834	0.5538
InfoXLM-Large	0.1061	0.4564	0.1526	0.0462	0.5168	0.1416
mBERT	0.3016	0.3379	0.3738	0.4825	0.4603	0.4952
RemBert	0.1536	0.3804	0.3646	0.2695	0.4961	0.4902
mDeBERTa-v3-base	0.3825	0.3962	0.4120	0.4681	0.4894	0.4827

In addition, not all models benefit from the selection of loss defined in Eq. 20. Table 5 gives the comparison between two loss functions when using different encoders and multilevel interactive module. The same model on different language pairs shows opposite effects which suggests that the loss function must be carefully designed.

Table 5. Results on Dev set of loss functions

Language pair	En-Zh		Zh-En	
loss type	MSE	MSE w/ sqrt	MSE	MSE w/ sqrt
XLM-RoBERTa-Large	0.3664	0.3943	0.4834	0.4540
InfoXLM-large	0.4564	0.4546	0.5168	0.5070
mBERT	0.3379	0.3025	0.4603	0.4754
RemBert	0.3804	0.3402	0.4961	0.5193
mDeBERTa-v3-base	0.3962	0.3766	0.4894	0.4978

4.4 Model Ensemble

According to the experiments of single model, we do a grid search on combinations of different models with high Pearson correlation coefficient on Dev set. Table 6 compares the results by using two different ensemble methods as described in Sect. 3.3.

Table 6. Results on Dev and online Test of ensembles

Language pair	En-Zh			Zh-En		
dataset	Dev	Online Test	Offline Test	Dev	Online Test	Offline Test
average	0.4712	0.5059	–	0.5743	0.5307	–
rank-weighted sum	0.4747	0.5120	0.3668	0.5690	0.5357	0.4687

We can see that allocating distinct weights to different models can perform better which implies that more adjustments on weights may surpass the current results. And our results are competitive even on offline Test set.

5 Conclusion

This paper describes our method for CCMT 2023 Quality Estimation Task on both English-to-Chinese and Chinese-to-English directions. With the help of PLMs and specially designed pretraining tasks, we can get better representations of *src* text and its *mt* text. The application of pretraining on generated HTER data helps model predict more accurate scores while *mlm* pretraining harms some

PLMs' ability to make better predictions. Both pretraining on HTER data and *mlm* way can further improve model performance in most cases. Since the prediction of HTER score requires taking account of the editing on word level, interactions between source words and translation words need to be modeled deeply to reflect the change of consistency semantically and grammatically. Experiment results show that our models can generate scores of higher Pearson correlation coefficient with true HTER scores when making deeper and multiple levels of representations interactive between *src* and its *mt*. When combining different levels of interactive modules on different language pairs, different PLMs show better or worse results which suggests that it is hard to design a universal module for various language pairs but using interactive modules always boosts the performance. We will leave it as future work. Moreover, the change of loss function increases Pearson correlation coefficient significantly on Dev set. Also, the ensemble method based on the rankings of models makes the prediction scores more relevant which indicates that it has much potential to explore the best combination of weights. Our models achieve competitive results in both English-to-Chinese and Chinese-to-English directions.

Acknowledgement. The participants would like to express heartfelt thanks to the committee and the organizers of the CCMT Quality Estimation Task. We would also like to show our gratitude to the reviewers for their invaluable suggestions. This work is supported by Transn IOL Technology Co., Ltd.

References

1. Specia, L., Shah, K., De Souza, J.G., Cohn, T.: QuEst-A translation quality estimation framework. In: Proceedings of the 51st Annual Meeting of the Association for Computational Linguistics: System Demonstrations, pp. 79–84, August 2013
2. Specia, L., Paetzold, G., Scarton, C.: Multi-level translation quality prediction with quest++. In: Proceedings of ACL-IJCNLP 2015 System Demonstrations, pp. 115–120, July 2015
3. Ive, J., Blain, F., Specia, L.: DeepQuest: a framework for neural-based quality estimation. In: Proceedings of the 27th International Conference on Computational Linguistics, pp. 3146–3157, August 2018
4. Kepler, F., Trénous, J., Treviso, M., Vera, M., Martins, A.F.T.: OpenKiwi: an open source framework for quality estimation. In: Proceedings of the 57th Annual Meeting of the Association for Computational Linguistics: System Demonstrations, pp. 117–122. Association for Computational Linguistics, Florence, Italy (2019)
5. Ranasinghe, T., Orasan, C., Mitkov, R: TransQuest: translation quality estimation with cross-lingual transformers. In: Proceedings of the 28th International Conference on Computational Linguistics, pp. 5070–5081. International Committee on Computational Linguistics, Barcelona, Spain (Online) (2020)
6. Rei, R., Stewart, C., Farinha, A.C., Lavie, A.: COMET: a neural framework for MT evaluation. In: Proceedings of the 2020 Conference on Empirical Methods in Natural Language Processing (EMNLP), pp. 2685–2702. Association for Computational Linguistics (2020)

7. Snover, M., Dorr, B., Schwartz, R., Micciulla, L., Makhoul, J.: A study of translation edit rate with targeted human annotation. In: Proceedings of the 7th Conference of the Association for Machine Translation in the Americas: Technical Papers, pp. 223–231 (2006)
8. Devlin, J., Chang, M.-W., Lee, K., Toutanova, K.: BERT: pre-training of deep bidirectional transformers for language understanding. In: Proceedings of the 2019 Conference of the North American Chapter of the Association for Computational Linguistics: Human Language Technologies, Volume 1 (Long and Short Papers), pp. 4171–4186. Association for Computational Linguistics, Minneapolis, Minnesota (2019)
9. Liu, Y., et al.: RoBERTa: A Robustly Optimized BERT Pretraining Approach (2019)
10. Vaswani, A., et al.: Attention is all you need. In: Advances in Neural Information Processing Systems, vol. 30 (2017)
11. Kim, H., Jung, H.Y., Kwon, H., Lee, J.H., Na, S.H.: Predictor-estimator: neural quality estimation based on target word prediction for machine translation. ACM Trans. Asian Low-Resource Lang. Inf. Process. (TALLIP) 17(1), 1–22 (2017)
12. Rei, R., et al.: CometKiwi: IST-unbabel 2022 submission for the quality estimation shared task. In: Proceedings of the Seventh Conference on Machine Translation (WMT), pp. 634–645. Association for Computational Linguistics, Abu Dhabi, United Arab Emirates (Hybrid) (2022)
13. Yang, R., Zhang, J., Gao, X., Ji, F., Chen, H.: Simple and effective text matching with richer alignment features. In: Proceedings of the 57th Annual Meeting of the Association for Computational Linguistics, pp. 4699–4709). Association for Computational Linguistics, Florence, Italy (2019)
14. Chen, Q., Zhu, X., Ling, Z.-H., Wei, S., Jiang, H., Inkpen, D.: Enhanced LSTM for natural language inference. In: Proceedings of the 55th Annual Meeting of the Association for Computational Linguistics (Volume 1: Long Papers), pp. 1657–1668. Association for Computational Linguistics, Vancouver, Canada (2017)
15. Hochreiter, S., Schmidhuber, J.: Long short-term memory. Neural Comput. 9(8), 1735–1780 (1997)
16. Specia, L., Farzindar, A.: Estimating machine translation post-editing effort with HTER. In: Proceedings of the Second Joint EM+/CNGL Workshop: Bringing MT to the User: Research on Integrating MT in the Translation Industry, pp. 33–43 (2010)
17. Tuan, Y.-L., El-Kishky, A., Renduchintala, A., Chaudhary, V., Guzmán, F., Specia, L.: Quality estimation without human-labeled data. In: Proceedings of the 16th Conference of the European Chapter of the Association for Computational Linguistics: Main Volume, pp. 619–625. Association for Computational Linguistics (2021)
18. Feng, F., Yang, Y., Cer, D., Arivazhagan, N., Wang, W.: Language-agnostic BERT sentence embedding. In: Proceedings of the 60th Annual Meeting of the Association for Computational Linguistics (Volume 1: Long Papers), pp. 878–891. Association for Computational Linguistics, Dublin, Ireland (2022)
19. He, P., Gao, J., Chen, W.: DeBERTaV3: improving DeBERTa using ELECTRA-style pre-training with gradient-disentangled embedding sharing. In: The Eleventh International Conference on Learning Representations (2022)

20. Chi, Z., et al.: InfoXLM: an information-theoretic framework for cross-lingual language model pre-training. In: Proceedings of the 2021 Conference of the North American Chapter of the Association for Computational Linguistics: Human Language Technologies, pp. 3576–3588. Association for Computational Linguistics (2021)
21. Conneau, A., et al.: Unsupervised cross-lingual representation learning at scale. In: Proceedings of the 58th Annual Meeting of the Association for Computational Linguistics, pp. 8440–8451. Association for Computational Linguistics (2020)
22. Chung, H.W., Fevry, T., Tsai, H., Johnson, M., Ruder, S.: Rethinking embedding coupling in pre-trained language models. In: International Conference on Learning Representations (2020)
23. Loshchilov, I., Hutter, F.: Decoupled weight decay regularization. In: International Conference on Learning Representations (2018)
24. Pytorch Homepage. https://pytorch.org/. Accessed 11 Sept 2023
25. Huggingface-transformers Homepage. huggingface.co/docs/transformers/index. Accessed 11 Sept 2023
26. SciPy Homepage. https://scipy.org/. Accessed 11 Sept 2023
27. Sacrebleu Homepage. https://github.com/mjpost/sacrebleu. Accessed 11 Sept 2023
28. mBART50 mt Model Page. https://huggingface.co/facebook/mbart-large-50-many-to-many-mmt. Accessed 11 Sept 2023
29. Helsinki-NLP's en-zh mt Model Page. https://huggingface.co/Helsinki-NLP/opus-mt-en-zh. Accessed 11 Sept 2023
30. Helsinki-NLP's zh-en mt Model Page. https://huggingface.co/Helsinki-NLP/opus-mt-zh-en. Accessed 11 Sept 2023
31. M2M100 Model Page. https://huggingface.co/facebook/m2m100_418M. Accessed 11 Sept 2023
32. NLLB-200 Model Page. https://huggingface.co/facebook/nllb-200-distilled-600M. Accessed 11 Sept 2023

HW-TSC's Neural Machine Translation System for CCMT 2023

Zhanglin Wu, Zhengzhe Yu, Zongyao Li, Daimeng Wei, Yuhao Xie,
Xiaoyu Chen, Hengchao Shang, Jiaxin Guo, Zhiqiang Rao, Shaojun Li,
Song peng, Lizhi Lei, Hao Yang(✉), and Yanfei Jiang

Huawei Translation Service Center, Beijing, China
{pengsong2,yanghao30}@huawei.com

Abstract. This paper presents Huawei Translation Service Center
(HW-TSC)'s submission to the machine translation tasks of the 19th
China Conference on Machine Translation (CCMT 2023). We participate in all machine translation tasks, including five bilingual machine
translation tasks, the Belt and Road low-resource language machine
translation task, Chinese-centric multilingual machine translation task
and Chinese→English zero-referencing machine translation task. Under
different machine translation tasks, we adopt different methods to train
the corresponding neural machine translation system. This paper mainly
explains the model structure, data size and training method adopted
by the translation systems, and gives the comparison of the evaluation
results under different training methods.

Keywords: CCMT 2023 · The Belt and Road · Low-resource ·
Chinese-centric · Multilingual · Zero-reference · Neural machine
translation

1 Introduction

Machine translation (MT) studies how to use machine to automatically translate one natural language (source language) to another natural language (target
language). Modern machine translation research has gone through rule-based
machine translation (RBMT) [1], statistical machine translation (SMT) [2], and
now the most mainstream neural machine translation (NMT) [3] based on deep
learning. NMT is based on the end-to-end neural network model (seq2seq), and
the core module has gradually evolved from the recurrent neural network (RNN)
[4] to the current mainstream Transformer architecture [5] based on the self-
attention mechanism. In recent years, NMT has made remarkable progress, especially in some specific domains or restricted scenarios, such as news translation
[6,7]. However, there are still many problems to be solved. For example, the
quality of the translation model for language pairs with scarce resources [8] is
low; the translation at the chapter level [9] is not coherent and smooth, etc.

In order to promote academic exchanges and contacts between domestic
and foreign scientific research units and related units in the industry, and

jointly promote the development of machine translation research and technology, CCMT2023 organizes a series of MT tasks[1]. We participate in all MT tasks, including five bilingual translation tasks, the Belt and Road low-resource language translation task, Chinese-centric multilingual translation task and Chinese→English zero-referencing translation task.

This paper describes the details of our NMT system for different translation tasks. The structure of this paper is as follows: Sect. 2 introduces the data size and data pre-processing process; Sect. 3 explains the system overview for different tasks; Sect. 4 illustrates the training methods; Sect. 5 presents the parameter settings and experimental results; Sect. 6 provides a systematic conclusion.

2   Dataset

2.1   Data Size

We strictly follow the requirements of CCMT 2023 outline to train the NMT systems. The outline requires that the primary system of other translation tasks should be derived from constrained training, except for low-resource language translation task.

Table 1 shows the training data size of each bilingual translation task after data pre-processing. These translation tasks include English→Chinese (en→zh), Chinese→English (zh→en), Mongolian→Chinese (mn→zh), Tibetan→Chinese (ti→zh) and Uygur→Chinese (uy→zh) translation tasks. It should be noted that in the en→zh and zh→en translation tasks, since the training data of WMT 2023 is shared with CCMT 2023, we additionally use the training data provided by WMT 2023 under the news task.

Table 1. Data size for each bilingual translation task after data pre-processing

	en→zh	zh→en	mn→zh	ti→zh	uy→zh
Bilingual	25.12M	25.12M	1.24M	0.97M	0.16 M
Source Monolingual	50M	50M	–	–	–
Target Monolingual	50M	50M	4.89M	4.89M	4.89 M

Table 2 shows the training data size of the Belt and Road low-resource language translation task after data pre-processing. These translation tasks include Chinese↔Czech (zh↔cs), Chinese↔Laos (zh↔lo), Chinese↔Mongolian (zh↔mn) and Chinese↔Vietnamese (zh↔vi) translation tasks. All the aforementioned translation tasks are unconstrained. Therefore, we employed three data set for each task during training. Firstly, we utilize a limited amount of

---

[1] http://sc.cipsc.org.cn/mt/conference/2023/tech-eval.

high-quality bilingual data provided by the official sources, and extract 2K sentences from them as the dev set. Secondly, for each low-resource language translation task mentioned above, we select corresponding English to minor language data as bridge data. These bilingual datasets officially provided by previous WMT and internet crawler data. Lastly, we incorporate monolingual Chinese and corresponding minority language data obtained from previous competitions and internet crawlers.

Table 2. Data size for each low-resource translation task after data pre-processing

	zh↔cs	zh↔lo	zh↔mn	zh↔vi
Bilingual	194K	195K	197K	193K
bridge	40M	3.61M	18.3M	7.2M
monolingual	40M	1.66M	26.2M	15M

Table 3 shows the training data size of Chinese-centric multilingual translation task after data pre-processing. This translation tasks involves multiple translation directions, include Chinese↔Hindi (zh↔hi), Chinese↔Kazakhstan (zh↔kk), Chinese↔Thai (zh↔th), Chinese↔Vietnamese (zh↔vi) and Chinese↔Uighur (zh↔ug). All the aforementioned translation directions are constrained as required by CCMT 2023 outline. Therefore, we exclusively utilize the official bilingual data and extract 2K sentences from each bilingual data as a dev set.

Table 3. Data size for multilingual translation task after data pre-processing

	zh↔hi	zh↔kk	zh↔th	zh↔vi	zh↔ug
Bilingual	500K	507K	506K	499K	491K

Table 4 shows the training data size of Zero-referencing translation task after data pre-processing. Our data is divided into two levels: sentence-level (sen-level) and document-level (doc-level). The data is composed of Opensubtitle, News crawl, and Common Crawl.

Table 4. Data size for Zero-referencing translation task after data pre-processing

	sen-level	doc-level
Bilingual	25.12M	5M
Source Monolingual	100M	50M
Target Monolingual	100M	50M

2.2 Data Pre-processing

The data pre-processing process is as follows:

- Remove duplicate sentences or sentence pairs.
- Remove invisible characters and xml escape characters.
- Convert full-width symbols to half-width symbols.
- Use jieba[2] to pre-segment Chinese sentences.
- Use mosesdecoder[3] to normalize English punctuation.
- Use opencc[4] to convert traditional Chinese to simplified Chinese.
- Use fasttext[5] to filter other language sentences in Chinese and English data.
- Use fast_align[6] to filter poorly aligned sentence pairs in high-resource bilingual.
- Split long sentences in monolingual data into multiple short sentences.
- Filter out sentences with more than 150 tokens in bilingual data.
- Filter out sentence pairs with token ratio greater than 4 or less than 0.25.
- When performing subword segmentation, joint Byte Pair Encoding[7] [10] is used for mn→zh, ti→zh and uy→zh translation tasks, and joint sentence-piece[8] [11] is used for other translation tasks. The vocabulary size of each task is 32K.

3 System Overview

3.1 Bilingual System

Transformer is the state-of-the-art model structure in recent MT evaluations. There are two parts of research to improve this kind: the first part uses wide networks (eg: Transformer-Big [5]), and the other part uses deeper language representations (eg: Deep Transformer [12]). For all five bilingual translation tasks, we combine these two improvements, adopting the Deep Transformer-Big [13] model structure to train the NMT system from scratch. Deep Transformer-Big uses pre-layer normalization, features 25-layer encoder, 6-layer decoder, 16-heads self-attention, 1024-dimensional word embedding and 4096-dimensional ffn embedding.

---

[2] https://github.com/fxsjy/jieba.
[3] https://github.com/moses-smt/mosesdecoder.
[4] https://github.com/BYVoid/OpenCC.
[5] https://github.com/facebookresearch/fastText.
[6] https://github.com/clab/fast_align.
[7] https://github.com/soaxelbrooke/python-bpe.
[8] https://github.com/google/sentencepiece.

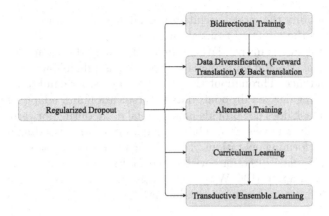

Fig. 1. The overall training flow chart of our NMT system for bilingual translation tasks.

Figure 1 shows the overall training flow chart of our translation system in bilingual translation tasks, including regularized dropout, bidirectional training, data diversification, forward translation, back translation, alternated training, curriculum learning and transductive ensemble learning. Since forward translation relies on source monolingual and mn→zh, ti→zh and uy→zh translation tasks do not provide source monolingual, we do not use forward translation on these three tasks. Furthermore, our choice of back translation methods varies across different tasks. For en→zh and zh→en tasks where forward translation is available, we use sampling back translation (ST) [14], and for other tasks we use tagged back translation (Tagged BT) [15].

3.2 Low-Resource System

For the unconstrained low-resource translation task, we refer to our previous work on WMT21 triangular translation shared task [16]. To address the issue of insufficient data for translating from Chinese to minor languages, we employ triangulation translation by incorporating English to minor languages data and combining it with Chinese→English translation models to construct bridging data for Chinese to minor language translation. This step is crucial in enabling us to obtain a sufficient amount of pseudo-bilingual data for Chinese to minor languages language pairs. Throughout the training process, we utilize various methods such as regularized dropout, forward translation and back translation.

3.3 Multilingual System

According to CCMT 2023 outline requirements for multilingual translation task, we integrate bidirectional data from all language directions and traine a single multi2multi model. To construct the model and data, we refer to Google's multilingual translation model [17]. The advantage of this approach is that we do not need to modify the model architecture. That is, we can use the same model architecture as the bilingual translation tasks.

To guide the model in translating different language directions, we followe the idea of Wu et al. [18]and add language tags such as "zh2hi" at the beginning of the source sentence. Throughout the training process, we employ various methods including regularized dropout, data diversification and adapter fine-tuning.

Since this task does not provide monolingual data, during forward translation and back translation, we split the bilingual data into corresponding monolingual data before performing operations. To mitigate interference between translations in different language directions within the multilingual translation model, we introduce the adapter [19]. We configure specific adapters for each language direction and fine-tune them using bilingual data.

3.4 Zero-Referencing System

The zero-referencing translation task refers to the scenario where pronouns are omitted in the original text, and the translation model is capable of accurately translating the missing pronouns. We employ the Doc2Doc [20,21] technique for discourse translation to address this issue. Firstly, we select document-level monolingual data from publicly available datasets such as WMT, which include news articles, movie subtitles, etc. Using the sentence-level model trained on the Chinese-English bilingual translation task, we utilize the document-level back translation (DocBT) method proposed in [22] to generate synthetic document-level bilingual data. Secondly, we integrate the data augmentation method with multi-resolution training mentioned in [23] and the approach of adding different separators between sentences within a document as mentioned in [23]. Furthermore, we conduct incremental training on the sentence-level model by combining the synthetic data with bilingual data.

We employ G-Transformer proposed in [24], which introduces the locality assumption as an inductive bias into the Transformer. This reduces the hypothesis space of attention from target to source. We train the G-Transformer model using bilingual data and the synthetic data generated by the DocBT method. The parameter configuration of the encoder and decoder models in G-transformer remains consistent with Deep Transformer-Big. Additionally, we employ group attention exclusively in the lower layers for local sentence representation, while utilizing combined attention in the top two layers to integrate local and global context information.

In this way, we obtain two document-level translation models: one is the original transformer, and the other is the G-transformer. Then, we select document-level Chinese monolingual data and use the document-level model for forward translation. We also incorporated the previously generated DocBT data into the training dataset. We further incrementally train the model by combining synthetic and bilingual data. Finally, we carefully select domain-specific data to train the final model using curriculum learning.

4   Method

4.1   Regularized Dropout

Dropout [25] is a widely used technique for regularizing deep neural network training, which is crucial to prevent over-fitting and improve the generalization ability of deep models. Dropout performs implicit ensemble by simply dropping a certain proportion of hidden units from the neural network during training, which may cause an unnegligible inconsistency between training and inference. Regularized Dropout[9] (R-Drop) [26] is a simple yet more effective alternative to regularize the training inconsistency induced by dropout. Concretely, in each mini-batch training, each data sample goes through the forward pass twice, and each pass is processed by a different sub model by randomly dropping out some hidden units. R-Drop forces the two distributions for the same data sample outputted by the two sub models to be consistent with each other, through minimizing the bidirectional Kullback-Leibler (KL) divergence [27] between the two distributions. That is, R-Drop regularizes the outputs of two sub models randomly sampled from dropout for each data sample in training. In this way, the inconsistency between the training and inference stage can be alleviated.

4.2   Bidirectional Training

Many studies have shown that pre-training can transfer the knowledge and data distribution, hence improving the generalization. Bidirectional training (BiT) [28] happens to be a simple and effective pre-training method for NMT. As shown in Fig. 2, bidirectional training is divided into two stages, the early stage bidirectionally updates model parameters, and then tune the model normally. To achieve bidirectional updating, we only need to reconstruct the training samples from "src→tgt" to "src+tgt→tgt+src" without any complicated model modifications. Notably, BiT does not increase any parameters or training steps, requiring the parallel data merely.

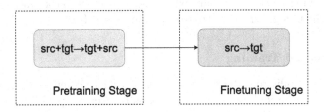

Fig. 2. Bidirectional training process for NMT.

---

[9] https://github.com/dropreg/R-Drop.

4.3 Data Diversification

Data Diversification (DD) [29] is a data augmentation method to boost NMT performance. It diversifies the training data by using the predictions of multiple forward and backward models and then merging them with the original dataset on which the final NMT model is trained. DD is applicable to all NMT models. It does not require extra monolingual data, nor does it add more computations and parameters. To conserve training resources, we only use one forward model and one backward model when using DD.

4.4 Forward Translation

Forward translation (FT), also known as self-training [30], is one of the most commonly used data augmentation methods. FT has proven effective for improving NMT performance by augmenting model training with synthetic parallel data. Generally, FT is performed in three steps: (1) randomly sample a subset from the large-scale source monolingual data; (2) use a "teacher" NMT model to translate the subset data into the target language to construct the synthetic parallel data; (3) combine the synthetic and authentic parallel data to train a "student" NMT model.

4.5 Back-Translation

An effective method to improve NMT with target monolingual data is to augment the parallel training data with back translation (BT) [31]. There are many works broaden the understanding of BT and investigates a number of methods to generate synthetic source sentences. Edunov et al. [14] find that back translations obtained via sampling or noised beam outputs are more effective than back translations generated by beam or greedy search in most scenarios. Caswell et al. [15] show that the main role of such noised beam outputs is not to diversify the source side, but simply to indicate to the model that the given source is synthetic. Therefore, they propose a simpler alternative to noised technique, Tagged BT. This method uses an extra token to mark back translated source sentences, which is generally outperform than noised BT.

4.6 Alternated Training

While synthetic bilingual data have demonstrated their effectiveness in NMT, adding more synthetic data often deteriorates translation performance since the synthetic data inevitably contains noise and erroneous translations. Alternated training (AT) [32] introduce authentic data as guidance to prevent the training of NMT models from being disturbed by noisy synthetic data. AT describes the synthetic and authentic data as two types of different approximations for the distribution of infinite authentic data, and its basic idea is to alternate synthetic and authentic data iteratively during training until the model converges. The training process of AT is shown in Fig. 3:

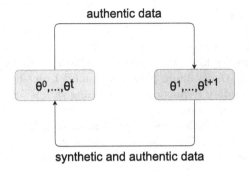

Fig. 3. Alternated training process for NMT.

4.7 Curriculum Learning

A practical curriculum learning (CL) [33] method should address two main questions: how to rank the training examples, and how to modify the sampling procedure based on this ranking. For ranking, we choose to estimate the difficulty of training samples according to their domain feature [34]. The calculation formula of domain feature is as follows, where θ_{in} represents an in-domain NMT model, and θ_{out} represents a out-of-domain NMT model.

$$q(x,y) = \frac{\log P(y|x;\theta_{in}) - \log P(y|x;\theta_{out})}{|y|} \tag{1}$$

For the sampling procedure, we adopt a probabilistic CL strategy[10] that takes advantage of the spirit of CL in a nondeterministic fashion without discarding the good practice of original standard training policy, like bucketing and mini-batching.

4.8 Transductive Ensemble Learning

Ensemble learning [35], which aggregates multiple diverse models for inference, is a common practice to improve the accuracy of machine learning tasks. However, it has been observed that the conventional ensemble methods only bring marginal improvement for NMT when individual models are strong or there are a large number of individual models. Transductive Ensemble Learning (TEL) [36] study how to effectively aggregate multiple NMT models under the transductive setting where the source sentences of the test set are known. TEL uses all individual models to translate the source test set into the target language space and then finetune a strong model on the translated synthetic data, which boosts strong individual models with significant improvement and benefits a lot from more individual models.

---

[10] https://github.com/kevinduh/sockeye-recipes/tree/master/egs/curriculum.

5   Experiments

We use Pytorch-based Fairseq [37] open-source framework to train NMT model, and use Adam optimizer [38] with $\beta1=0.9$ and $\beta2=0.98$ to guide the parameter optimization. During the training phase, each model uses 8 GPUs for training, batch size is 2048, update frequency is 4, learning rate is 5e-4, label smoothing rate is 0.1 and warm-up steps is 4000. We set dropout to 0.1 for high-resource translation tasks and 0.3 for low-resource translation tasks respectively. In addition, when applying R-Drop for training, we follow the setting of Liang et al. [26], using reg_label_smoothed_cross_entropy as the loss function, and set reg-alpha to 5. Then, we use SacreBLEU [39] to evaluate the overall translation quality of each model.

5.1   Bilingual System Evaluation Results

5.1.1   En→zh & Zh→en

On en→zh and zh→en translation tasks, we use BiT and R-Drop to build a strong baseline system. Subsequently, we adopt the data augmentation methods of DD, FT and ST to improve the translation quality of baseline System. Next, we use AT guide model training with authentic bilingual data. Then, we use CL for domain adaptation. Finally, we train multiple systems and integrate them using TEL as the final translation system.

Table 5. BLEU scores of en→zh & zh→en NMT system

test set	en→zh		zh→en	
	WMT 2021	CCMT 2021	WMT 2021	CCMT 2021
BiT R-Drop baseline	34.20	47.80	26.23	31.23
+ DD, FT & ST	34.72	50.03	27.68	32.25
+ AT	34.89	50.79	28.06	35.06
+ CL	35.12	53.05	30.34	39.93
+ TEL	**36.15**	**53.63**	**32.23**	**40.22**

Table 5 shows the evaluation results of en→zh and zh→en translation systems. Compared with the baseline system, the final en→zh and zh→en translation systems improves significantly on WMT 2021 and CCMT 2021 test sets.

5.1.2   Mn→zh, Ti→zh & Uy→zh

On mn→zh, ti→zh and uy→zh translation tasks, we also use BiT and R-Drop to build a strong baseline system. The subsequent training method is similar to en→zh and zh→en translation tasks. The only difference is that we adopt DD and Tagged BT in the data augmentation stage, which is due to the lack of source language monolingual for these three tasks. Table 6 is the evaluation results of mn→zh, ti→zh and uy→zh translation systems on CCMT 2021 test set. Overall, the final translation systems for all three tasks improves significantly compared to the baseline system.

Table 6. BLEU scores of mn→zh, ti→zh and uy→zh translation system

	mn→zh	ti→zh	uy→zh
BiT R-Drop baseline	55.57	47.69	43.89
+ DD & Tagged BT	59.03	52.10	50.76
+ AT	61.19	52.84	51.37
+ CL	62.32	54.71	51.95
+ TEL	**63.02**	**56.15**	**52.79**

5.2   Low-Resource System Evaluation Results

For the unconstrained low-resource translation task, we first train a baseline model using a small amount of high-quality bilingual data provided by official sources. Then, We use a en→zh model to build bridge data for model enhancement training. Finally, we achieve optimal performance by incorporating monolingual data into the model through forward translation (FT) and back translation (BT). Table 7 presents the evaluation results of our low-resource translation system. After introducing bridge data and synthetic data, a significant improvement in model quality can be observed, such as cs→zh exhibiting an increase of more than 10 BLEU. It also shows that the baseline model underperforms due to the limited amount of bilingual data.

Table 7. BLEU scores of low-resource translation system

	zh→cs	cs→zh	zh→lo	lo→zh	zh→mn	mn→zh	zh→vi	vi→zh
R-Drop baseline	18.10	34.21	20.50	32.81	29.80	30.95	41.25	39.49
+ bridge data	32.57	53.10	30.43	42.10	31.82	31.40	55.15	50.09
+ FT & BT	**34.09**	**54.60**	**34.29**	**42.70**	**32.39**	**33.17**	**56.90**	**54.71**

5.3   Multilingual System Evaluation Results

Regarding the multilingual translation task, due to limited data, we conduct multiple rounds training. Initially, we train a multi2multi model as the baseline by integrating bilingual data provided by official sources. Subsequently, we introduce the adapter structure and fine-tune each direction using bilingual data. In addition, we use data diversification (DD) to construct synthetic data corresponding to bilingual data for training. Thereafter, we repeated the above procedure to complete the second round of training. Finally, we use bilingual data to perform final adapter fine-tuning (AF).

Table 8 presents the evaluation results of our multilingual translation system, which demonstrates the effective implementation of our methods. The final model has exhibited significant improvements compared to the baseline model. We also note that the quality improvement in the second round of intensive training is relatively limited compared to the first round. This shows that we have hit a data bottleneck, considering we have less than 50k bilingual data per language direction. Particularly in the last round of adapter fine-tuning, we can observe a very limited quality improvement, and certain language directions have even experienced a decline. We have also observed significant overall improvements in the translation from all minor languages to Chinese. However, there has been a relatively smaller improvement in the translation quality from Chinese to minor languages. We believe this could be attributed to the gains in target language direction being consistent across multilingual models.

Table 8. BLEU scores of multilingual translation system

	zh→hi	hi→zh	zh→kk	kk→zh	zh→th	th→zh	zh→vi	vi→zh	zh→ug	ug→zh
R-Drop baseline	30.82	39.41	30.35	32.60	46.20	21.92	35.72	29.14	40.11	43.06
+ AF	31.24	40.39	30.86	33.07	46.23	22.08	35.96	30.14	40.14	44.65
+ DD	31.60	44.43	31.14	34.39	47.70	22.72	36.31	35.17	40.37	46.19
+ 2nd AF & DD	32.04	44.91	32.06	35.05	**48.30**	23.20	37.06	**35.80**	40.38	**46.93**
+ 3nd AF	**32.28**	**45.06**	**32.37**	**35.13**	48.20	**23.34**	**37.16**	35.71	**40.99**	46.84

5.4   Zero-Referencing System Evaluation Results

By adding different tags between sentences, we are able to achieve sentence-level alignment between source and translated texts. Therefore, we primarily use sentence-level BLEU to evaluate the quality of our model.

Table 9. BLEU scores of Zero-referencing translation system

	Movie Subtitle	Web Fiction
BiT R-Drop baseline	16.8	6.3
+ DocBT	19.2	12.0
+ FT & ST	20.7	12.3
+ CL	21.5	13.2
G-Trans	19.5	12.1
+ FT & ST	20.8	12.2
+ CL	21.4	13.5
Ensemble	**21.5**	**13.6**

Table 9 presents the evaluation results of our system on the movie subtitle and web fiction dev sets. It can be observed that the bilingual baseline model (BIT R-Drop baseline) performs relatively poorly, especially in the web fiction dev set. However, both the original Transformer and G-Transformer (G-Trans) models show significant improvements with DocBT. Further enhancements by forward translation (FT) and sampling back translation (ST) make the model highly competitive. Even after curriculum learning (CL), these models still show some improvement. Ensembling the two models yields limited gains in performance. Due to some confusion during the implementation of the official metric provided by aZPT, we do not provide the accuracy of zero-pronoun translations.

6 Conclusion

This paper introduces HW-TSC's NMT system for CCMT 2023. In general, we participate in all machine translation tasks, including five bilingual machine translation tasks, the Belt and Road low-resource language machine translation task, Chinese-centric multilingual machine translation task and Chinese→English zero-referencing machine translation task. our NMT system is constructed based on the Transformer architecture and trained by a series of methods. To this end, we conduct a lot of experiments, and the experimental results show that these methods are effective.

References

1. Shiwen, Y., Xiaojing, B.: Rule-based machine translation. Routledge Encyclopedia of Translation Technology. Routledge, pp. 224–238 (2014)
2. Lopez, A.: Statistical machine translation. ACM Comput. Surv. (CSUR) **40**(3), 1–49 (2008)
3. Bahdanau, D., Cho, K.H., Bengio, Y.: Neural machine translation by jointly learning to align and translate. In: 3rd International Conference on Learning Representations, ICLR 2015 (2015)
4. Medsker, L.R., Jain, L.C.: Recurrent neural networks. Design Appli. **5** 64–67 (2001)
5. Vaswani, A., et al.: Attention is all you need. In: Advances in Neural Information Processing Systems 30 (2017)
6. Wei, D., et al.: Hw-tsc's participation in the wmt 2021 news translation shared task. In: Proceedings of the Sixth Conference on Machine Translation (2021)
7. Wei, D., et al.: Hw-tsc's submissions to the wmt 2022 general machine translation shared task. In: Proceedings of the Seventh Conference on Machine Translation, Online. Association for Computational Linguistics(2022)
8. Li, S., et al.: HW-TSC systems for WMT22 very low resource supervised MT Task. In: Proceedings of the Seventh Conference on Machine Translation. Association for Computational Linguistics (2022)
9. Miculicich, L., et al.: Document level neural machine translation with hierarchical attention networks. In: Proceedings of the Conference on Empirical Methods in Natural Language Processing (EMNLP). No. CONF (2018)

10. Sennrich, R., Haddow, B., Birch, A.: Neural machine translation of rare words with subword units. In: Proceedings of the 54th Annual Meeting of the Association for Computational Linguistics (Volume 1: Long Papers), pp. 1715–1725 (2016)

11. Kudo, T., Richardson, J.: SentencePiece: a simple and language independent subword tokenizer and detokenizer for Neural Text Processing. In: Proceedings of the 2018 Conference on Empirical Methods in Natural Language Processing: System Demonstrations (2018)

12. Wang, Q., Li, B., Xiao, T., et al.: Learning deep transformer models for machine translation. In: Proceedings of the 57th Annual Meeting of the Association for Computational Linguistics, pp. 1810–1822 (2019)

13. Wu, Z., et al.: Multi-strategy enhanced neural machine translation for chinese minority languages. In: Machine Translation: 18th China Conference, CCMT 2022, Lhasa, China, 6–10 August 2022, Revised Selected Papers. Springer Nature Singapore, Singapore (2022). https://doi.org/10.1007/978-981-19-7960-6_4

14. Edunov, S., Ott, M., Auli, M., et al.: Understanding back-translation at scale. In: Proceedings of the 2018 Conference on Empirical Methods in Natural Language Processing, pp. 489–500 (2018)

15. Caswell, I., Chelba, C., Grangier, D.: Tagged back-translation. In: Proceedings of the Fourth Conference on Machine Translation (Volume 1: Research Papers), pp. 53–63 (2019)

16. Li, Z., Wei, D., Shang, H., et al.: Hw-tsc's participation in the WMT 2021 triangular MT shared task. In: Proceedings of the Sixth Conference on Machine Translation, pp. 325–330 (v)

17. Johnson, M., Schuster, M., Le, Q.V., et al.: Google's multilingual neural machine translation system: enabling zero-shot translation. Trans. Assoc. Comput. Lingu. 5, 339–351 (2017)

18. Wu, L., et al.: Language tags matter for zero-shot neural machine translation. In: Findings of the Association for Computational Linguistics: ACL-IJCNLP 2021 (2021)

19. Bapna, A., Firat, O.: Simple, scalable adaptation for neural machine translation. In: Proceedings of the 2019 Conference on Empirical Methods in Natural Language Processing and the 9th International Joint Conference on Natural Language Processing (EMNLP-IJCNLP) (2019)

20. Zhang, J., et al.: Improving the transformer translation model with document-level context. In: Proceedings of the 2018 Conference on Empirical Methods in Natural Language Processing (2018)

21. Liu, Y., Gu, J., Goyal, N., et al.: Multilingual denoising pre-training for neural machine translation. Trans. Assoc. Comput. Lingu. 8, 726–742 (2020)

22. Junczys-Dowmunt, M.: Microsoft translator at WMT 2019: towards large-scale document-level neural machine translation. WMT 2019, 225 (2019)

23. Sun, Z., et al.: Rethinking document-level neural machine translation. In: Findings of the Association for Computational Linguistics: ACL 2022 (2022)

24. Bao, G.,, et al.: G-transformer for document-level machine translation. In: Proceedings of the 59th Annual Meeting of the Association for Computational Linguistics and the 11th International Joint Conference on Natural Language Processing (Volume 1: Long Papers) (2021)

25. Hinton, G.E., NitishSrivastava, A.K., Salakhutdinov, I.S.R.R.: Improving neural networks by preventing co-adaptation of feature detectors

26. Wu, L., Li, J., Wang, Y., et al.: R-Drop: regularized dropout for neural networks. In: Advances in Neural Information Processing Systems (2021)

27. Van Erven, T., Harremos, P.: Rényi divergence and Kullback-Leibler divergence. IEEE Trans. Inf. Theory **60**(7), 3797–3820 (2014)
28. Ding, L., Wu, D., Tao, D.: Improving neural machine translation by bidirectional training. In: Proceedings of the 2021 Conference on Empirical Methods in Natural Language Processing (2021)
29. Nguyen, X., et al.: Data diversification: a simple strategy for neural machine translation. Adv. Neural Inform. Process. Syst. **33**, 10018–10029 (2020)
30. Abdulmumin, I., Galadanci, B.S., Isa, A.: Enhanced back-translation for low resource neural machine translation using self-training. In: ICTA 2020. CCIS, vol. 1350, pp. 355–371. Springer, Cham (2021). https://doi.org/10.1007/978-3-030-69143-1_28
31. Sennrich, Rico, Barry Haddow, and Alexandra Birch. "Improving Neural Machine Translation Models with Monolingual Data." Proceedings of the 54th Annual Meeting of the Association for Computational Linguistics (Volume 1: Long Papers). 2016
32. Jiao, R., Yang, Z., Sun, M., et al.: alternated training with synthetic and authentic data for neural machine translation. In: Findings of the Association for Computational Linguistics: ACL-IJCNLP 2021, pp. 1828–1834 (2021)
33. Zhang, X., et al.: Curriculum learning for domain adaptation in neural machine translation. In: Proceedings of the 2019 Conference of the North American Chapter of the Association for Computational Linguistics: Human Language Technologies, Volume 1 (Long and Short Papers) (2019)
34. Wang, W., et al.: Learning a multi-domain curriculum for neural machine translation. In: Proceedings of the 58th Annual Meeting of the Association for Computational Linguistics (2020)
35. Garmash, E., Monz, C.: Ensemble learning for multi-source neural machine translation. In: Proceedings of COLING 2016, the 26th International Conference on Computational Linguistics: Technical Papers, pp. 1409–1418 (2016)
36. Wang, Y., et al.: Transductive ensemble learning for neural machine translation. In: Proceedings of the AAAI Conference on Artificial Intelligence, vol. 34(04) (2020)
37. Ott, M., Edunov, S., Baevski, A., et al.: fairseq: a fast, extensible toolkit for sequence modeling. In: Proceedings of the 2019 Conference of the North American Chapter of the Association for Computational Linguistics (Demonstrations), pp. 48–53 (2019)
38. Kingma, D.P., Ba, J.L.: Adam: A Method for Stochastic Optimization (2015)
39. Post, M.: A call for clarity in reporting BLEU scores. In: Proceedings of the Third Conference on Machine Translation: Research Papers, pp. 186–191 (2018)

CCMT2023 Tibetan-Chinese Machine Translation Evaluation Technical Report

Kalzang Gyatso[1], Peizhuo Liu[2], Yi Jing[2], Yinqiao Li[2], Nyima Tashi[1(✉)], Tong Xiao[2], and Jingbo Zhu[2]

[1] Tibetan Language Information Technology Ministry of Education Engineering Research Center, Tibet University, Tibet, China
nmzx@utibet.edu.com
[2] NLP Lab, Northeastern University, Shenyang, China
{xiaotong,zhujingbo}@mail.neu.edu.com

Abstract. This report presents the evaluation results of the Tibetan-Chinese machine translation task in the 19th Machine Translation Conference (CCMT2023) by Tibetan Language Information Technology Ministry of Education Engineering Research Center and NLP Lab at Northeastern University. This system uses data augmentation, ensemble and iterative Fine-tune to experiment with Tibetan-Chinese machine translation. The results showed that compared with the baseline model, the method used in this system can improve the performance of the translation quality.

Keywords: Tibetan-Chinese machine translation · Segmentation · Data augmentation

1 Introduction

In a multilingual society, machine translation plays a vital role in helping people overcome language barriers and promoting cross-cultural communication and understanding. The development of Tibetan-to-Chinese machine translation task not only facilitates communication and understanding between Chinese and Tibetan languages but also holds significant importance in advancing machine translation technology for minority language translation. This report provides an overview of the participation of Tibetan Language Information Technology Ministry of Education Engineering Research Center and NLP Lab in the 2023 evaluation of machine translation for Tibetan-Chinese machine translation. Our experiments were conducted using the Transformer base as the baseline model, with Transformer Big, ODE Transformer, and Transformer- DLCL as the primary models. Various techniques such as data augmentation, model ensemble, and iterative Fine-tuning were employed in the experiments.

2 Data Processing

2.1 Data

Training Set

The training set of our system is provided by the official source, comprising 1,157,959 sentence pairs of Tibetan to Chinese translation in various domains. This training set is used to train our system, enabling it to comprehend and process Tibetan to Chinese translation tasks effectively.

Validation Set

The verification set of this system consists of the merged verification set in 2019, the verification set in 2020 and the verification set in 2021, which contains 2198 pieces of bilingual data in total. Validation set data will be used to evaluate the translation quality and stability of the system in different time periods.

Test Set

Test set of this system contains 10000 Tibetan sentences, most of which are paragraph-level long sentences. Considering that the length of training data does not match the length of test data, this system carries out clause operation on test data.

We choose test set of this system adopts the official 2017 test suite, which contains 729 pieces of data from four different translation versions, named TEST1, TEST2, TEST3 and TEST4 respectively. This portion of the test set is used during model training to simulate the real test set and assess the performance of our model.

2.2 Data Preprocessing

Authentic Data

Preprocessing

In this system, we performed various preprocessing steps on the original corpus of the Train set, consisting of 1.15 million sentences. These steps included normalization, length filtering, converting full-angle to half-angle characters, removing illegal characters, case conversion, Chinese simplification, and removing excessively long words or sentence pairs. After preprocessing, we deduplicated the data and selected 944,310 sentences of higher quality for training. These preprocessing steps aimed to improve data quality, consistency, and establish a solid foundation for subsequent training and model construction.

Considering the disparity in length between the training and test data, this system applies clause operations to the test data. In Chinese writing, sentence boundaries are typically identified by commas, periods, semicolons, and other symbols, while in Tibetan, wedge symbols like " ", " ", and " " are commonly used to indicate the end of phrases, sentences, and chapters[1]. The Tibetan wedge symbol " " serves multiple functions, such as pause, comma, exclamation point, and full stop, similar to how these functions are expressed by different punctuation marks in Chinese. However, the use of the Tibetan wedge symbol " ྄" for sentence boundary recognition introduces ambiguities and functional uncertainties, making it challenging to accurately identify Tibetan sentence boundaries. To address this issue, the system employs a set of rules for clause operations on Tibetan test sentences.

For tokenization, we utilize the Jieba[1] word segmentation tool to segment Chinese sentences. As for Tibetan data, we employ a segmentation system based on Bi-LSTM + CRF [2, 3], which is trained on 160,000 Tibetan segmentation data. This word segmentation system enables effective segmentation of Tibetan data, providing an accurate and reliable foundation for subsequent translation tasks.

Synthetic Data

Data augmentation is commonly used technology in machine translation tasks, which aims to increase the diversity and quantity of training data and improve the generalization ability of models by transforming and expanding the original data [4]. Data enhancement can effectively prevent model over-fitting and improve the robustness of the model in different scenarios.

Back Translation

Back translation technology, widely used in natural language processing, employs a machine translation model to translate text from a source language to a target language and then translates it back to the source language [5]. This process generates a series of sentences related to the original text, enhancing the diversity and coverage of the dataset. By applying back translation to the Chinese-Tibetan machine translation task, our system successfully generates a substantial amount of pseudo-data, enriching the corpus resources for training the model and further improving system performance. Preprocessed Chinese monolingual data amounting to 4 million sentences are used for back translation, resulting in over 4 million Tibetan-Chinese bilingual sentence pairs that expand the original data.

On 944,310 bilingual sentence pairs, we utilize three models, namely Ode Transformer, Transformer-DLCL, and Transformer Big, for reverse translation from the target language to the source language. We average the parameters from the last five checkpoints of each model. These three parametric averaged models are then integrated, and the integrated model is employed for reverse translation of monolingual target language (Chinese).

For the more than 4 million bilingual pseudo-data, we conduct a series of preprocessing steps, including data standardization, length ratio filtering, conversion of full-width characters to half-width characters, removal of illegal characters, case conversion, conversion of traditional Chinese to simplified Chinese, and removal of excessively long or short sentence pairs. Following these steps, we perform duplicate removal operations, resulting in a final dataset of 1.8 million bilingual pseudo-data.

---

[1] https://github.com/fxsjy/jieba

Data Filtering
BLEU [6] is often used as an index to evaluate the quality of generated pseudo-data in the research of pseudo-data screening. Firstly, we use monolingual data in 1.8 million pseudo-data to translate through forward fusion model, and then calculate the BLEU value between the translated results and the original monolingual data. Then, according to the samples with different BLEU values, we form alternative pseudo-data sets, including 290,000, 410,000, 500,000 and 1 million pseudo-data, respectively.

XenC [7] is an open source tool for data selection in natural language processing. By calculating the cross-entropy scores of sentences in the domain corpus and out-of-domain corpus, the tool scores the data with strong domain correlation, and can select the data with strong domain correlation from the pseudo-data. Considering the domain deviation of monolingual data in the target language used in this paper, this system filters 1 million pieces of data from 1.85 million synthetic data through XenC tool and adds them to the alternative synthetic data set.

3   Model

3.1   Model Select

This system chooses Transformer base as the baseline model, and further chooses Transformer Big [8],Transformer-DLCL [9] and ODE Transformer [10] as the main models of the system. By means of parameter averaging and model integration, these three models are tested and compared.

Transformer Big
We introduced Transformer Big as a deeper, more complex model in the hope of achieving better performance in the task. Transformer Big adds more layers and a larger number of hidden units on the basis of Transformer base to enhance the expression ability and learning ability of the model.

Transformer-DLCL
The Transformer-DLCL leveraged direct links to all preceding layers, facilitating efficient access to lower-level representations within a deep stack. To assign a linear weight to each incoming layer, an additional weight matrix W was employed. This approach can be mathematically expressed as follows:

$$\Psi(y0,\ y1\ldots yl) = \sum\nolimits_{k=0}^{n} W_k^{(l+1)} LN(y_k) \tag{1}$$

Equation 1 provided a mechanism to acquire insights into the prefere1nces of layers at different levels in the stack, with $\Psi(y0, y1\ldots yl)$ denoting the amalgamation of representations from previous layers. Furthermore, this methodology is agnostic to the model architecture, allowing seamless integration with either the pre-norm Transformer or pre-norm Transformer-RPR to achieve further enhancements.

ODE Transformer
ODE Transformer is a variant based on ODE (Ordinary Differential Equation). By introducing the concepts of continuous time and discrete time into Transformer architecture, it realizes more continuous and smooth state transition and modeling ability. This

continuous-time modeling method is helpful to deal with long-distance dependencies and improve the modeling ability and translation quality of models. The parameters used by the three models mentioned above are listed in the Table 1.

Table 1. Selected Model and Relevant Parameters

Transformer Depth	Hidden Size	Filter Size	Batch Size	Update Freq
Transformer-DLCL	6	512	2048	4096
ODE Transformer	30	512	2048	2048
Transformer Big	30	512	2048	2048

3.2   Model Ensemble

Model ensemble combines predictions from multiple independent models to improve overall performance, accuracy, stability, and robustness. In our system, three distinct models (Transformer Big, Transformer-DLCL, and ODE Transformer) are trained, and their parameters are averaged. This yields the average parameters of the ensemble model, enhancing its performance and generalization ability. Evaluation is done using test or validation datasets to assess their effectiveness. Parameter averaging and model integration lead to more stable predictions and improved system performance.

3.3   Iterative Fine-Tuning

Iterative Fine-tuning is a method in machine learning and deep learning that optimizes the model through multiple iterations. It involves training a basic model, evaluating the results, Fine-tuning certain parameters or layers based on the evaluation, and repeating this process until the desired performance or convergence is achieved. This approach gradually improves the model's adaptation to complex tasks and specific datasets, enhancing its performance and generalization ability.

In order to further optimize our three models, we selected 1000 pairs of sentences from the 2022 test set for Fine-tuning. Each model underwent one round of Fine-tuning using these selected pairs. The purpose of Fine-tuning is to enhance the translation performance of the models in a specific domain, enabling them to better adapt to the data in the test set. Through this process, we aim to achieve more accurate and fluent translation results that meet the translation requirements in a comprehensive domain.

4   Experiment

4.1   Experimental Environment

We have implemented our model using Fairseq version 0.60, utilizing eight RTX 2080 Ti GPUs for accelerated computation.

4.2 Experimental Setup

We improved the Transformer-base model by adjusting its depth or width, increasing layers and hidden layer size. We used Adam optimizer and gradient accumulation every two steps to save GPU memory. Generally, 30 epochs yielded satisfactory results with consistent performance on the validation set.

For each model, we configured the number of warmup steps to be 10,000, based on improved performance on the validation set, and set the learning rate to 0.002. Additionally, to further expedite the training process, we employed FP16 mixed precision training, listed in the Table 2.

Table 2. Experimental setup.

	Base	Dense	Big	Ode
Emb_dim	512	512	1024	1024
Encoder_layer	6	25 (with norm)	6	6 (with norm)
Decoder_layer	6	6 (with norm)	6	6 (with norm)
Dropout	0.1	0.1	0.3	0.3
Label_smoothing	0.1	0.1	0.1	0.1
Optimizer	Adam	Adam	Adam	Adam

5   Results and Analysis

Initially, we conducted experiments on data selection and evaluated the performance of three types of preprocessed data on the 2017 test set using different Tibetan word segmentation strategies. The experimental findings indicate that Bi-LSTM + CRF performs the best for Tibetan word segmentation, the results are shown in Table3.

Table 3. The Impact of Tokenization System on Translation Performance

Data	2017 Test1	2017 Test2	2017 Test3	2017 Test4
rule-based	35.74	47.37	60.53	34.12
Bi-LSTM + CRF + rule	36.74	49.35	63.89	33.42
Bi-LSTM + CRF + <unk>	36.86	49.41	63.90	33.64

We trained the model using preprocessed and non-preprocessed training data separately, and then tested it on the test set. The results (Table 4) showed that the preprocessed data outperformed the non-preprocessed data.

Table 4. The Impact of Preprocessing on Model Performance

Data	2017 Test1	2017 Test2	2017 Test3	2017 Test4
Preprocessed	36.86	49.41	63.90	33.64
Non Preprocess	36.54	48.99	62.87	33.35

Table 5. The Impact of BPE Tokenization Granularity on Model Performance

BPE granularity	2017 Test1	2017 Test2	2017 Test3	2017 Test4
25K	35.74	47.37	60.53	34.12
32K	34.24	45.93	58.97	33.50

We used big Transformer to test the BPE segmentation strength of 25K and 32K on four test sets in 2017, and the results (Table 5) showed that 25K performed better than 32K on our data set.

For the selection of warmup and Learning rates, we cross-validated with Big Transformer in warmup 8000, 10000, 16000 and Learning rates 0.01 0.0015 0.002, and finally selected 10000 and 0.002 with higher blue as parameters in four test sets in 2017, the results are shown in the Table 6.

Table 6. The Impact of Warmup and Learning Rate Selection on Performance

Learning rates	warmup	2017 Test1	2017 Test2	2017 Test3	2017 Test4
0.001	8000	35.19	47.43	61.00	33.19
0.001	10000	34.65	46.45	59.89	33.35
0.001	10000	34.27	45.82	58.41	33.62
0.0015	8000	35.10	47.07	61.03	32.83
0.0015	10000	35.43	47.39	61.16	33.19
0.0015	16000	35.47	46.73	59.93	34.00
0.002	8000	35.13	46.98	60.79	33.47
0.002	10000	35.30	47.20	61.04	33.40
0.002	16000	34.24	45.93	58.97	33.50

After configuring data and model parameters, we trained three separate models. Averaging their parameters from the last five checkpoints, we evaluated their performance on the test set. Combining them as an Ensemble Model, we observed superior performance compared to individually trained models, the results are shown in the Table 7.

Table 7. The Impact of Model Ensembling on Translation Performance

BPE granularity	2017 Test1	2017 Test2	2017 Test3	2017 Test4
Transformer base	36.27	48.42	61.86	34.42
ODE Transformer	36.45	48.64	62.64	33.83
Transformer-DLCL	36.75	49.37	63.63	33.68
Transformer Big	36.91	48.44	62.00	34.26
Ensemble (ODE/DLCL/Big)	37.02	49.66	63.58	34.48

We tested the Transformer-DLCL model with synthetic data of various magnitudes and merging approaches. The results (Table 8) showed that adding carefully selected synthetic data did not significantly improve performance on the 2017 test set, and there was even a slight decrease. However, some performance improvement was observed on the validation set. Additionally, experimenting with two sets of synthetic data with " <bt>" tags and original data fusion did not effectively improve our dataset. (Note: All experiments in the table present the results obtained by training with the combined real data and the labeled synthetic data.)

Table 8. The Impact of Synthetic Data and <bt> Tags on Model Performance

Synthetic Data	2017 Test1	2017 Test2	2017 Test3	2017 Test4	Valid
290,000	35.9	47.44	60.9	33.41	37.27
290,000 with <bt>	35.82	47.57	61.29	33.39	36.82
410,000	35.9	47.44	60.9	33.41	36.99
410,000 with <bt>	35.73	47.09	60.51	37.35	37.35
500,000	35.93	47.56	61.14	34.01	37.38
1 million	35.08	45.40	57.47	34.25	37.96

6 Summary

We used the Transformer base model as the baseline and conducted extensive experiments in data selection, data augmentation, model selection, and model ensemble to improve its performance. We achieved positive results in data and model selection as well as model ensemble. However, data augmentation techniques (synthetic data) did not significantly improve our overall model on the 2017 test set due to poor micro-data quality and domain biases. To address domain bias, we employed XenC, a domain data selection tool, to select 1,000,000 domain-specific sentence pairs from synthetic data. These pairs were merged with the real corpus for model training, and submitted the results using this model.

Through this evaluation task, we conducted in-depth research on the performance and effectiveness of our Tibetan to Chinese machine translation system. The evaluation results showcase the performance of our system in terms of translation quality and usability.

Acknowledgments. This work was supported in part by the National Key R&D Program of China (2022ZD0116101). This work also supported in part by the National Science Foundation of China (No. 62276056), the National Key R&D Program of China, the China HTRD Center Project (No. 2020AAA0107904), the Natural Science Foundation of Liaoning Province of China (2022-KF-16–01), the Yunnan Provincial Major Science and Technology Special Plan Projects (No. 202103AA080015), the Fundamental Research Funds for the Central Universities (Nos. N2216016, N2216001, and N2216002), and the Program of Introducing Talents of Discipline to Universities, Plan 111 (No. B16009).

References

1. Phuchong, T.: On the Tibetan Traditional Punctuations and its Stand-ardization (2019)
2. Shi, X., Chen, Z., Wang, H., Yeung, D-Y., Wong, W., Woo, W.: Convolutional LSTM Network: A Machine Learning Approach for Precipitation Nowcasting (2015)
3. Lafferty, J., McCallum, A., Pereira, F.: Conditional Random Fields: Probabilistic Models for Segmenting and Labeling Sequence Data
4. Ranathunga, S., Lee, E-SA., Skenduli, M.P., Shekhar, R., Alam, M., Kaur, R.: Neural Machine Translation for Low-Resource Languages: A Survey (2021)
5. Xiao, T., Zhu, J.: Machine Translation: Foundations and Models (2020)
6. Papineni, K., Roukos, S., Ward, T., Zhu, W-J.: Bleu: a method for automatic evaluation of machine translation. In: Proceedings of the 40th Annual Meeting of the Association for Computational Linguistics. Association for Computational Linguistics, Philadelphia, Pennsylvania, USA, pp 311–318 (2002)
7. Rousseau, A.: XenC: an open-source tool for data selection in natural language processing. Prague Bull. Math. Ling. **100**, 73–82 (2013). https://doi.org/10.2478/pralin-2013-0013
8. Vaswani, A., et al.: Attention Is All You Need (2017)
9. Wang, Q., Li, B., Xiao, T., Zhu, J., Li, C., Wong, D.F., Chao, L.S.: Learning deep transformer models for machine translation. In: Proceedings of the 57th Annual Meeting of the Association for Computational Linguistics. Association for Computational Linguistics, Florence, Italy, pp 1810–1822 (2019)
10. Li, B., et al.: ODE transformer: an ordinary differential equation-inspired model for sequence generation (2022)

Korean-Chinese Machine Translation Method Based on Independent Language Features

Fan Liu[1,2], Yahui Zhao[2(✉)], Guozhe Jin[2], Xinghua Lu[1], Zhejun Jin[3], and Rongyi Cui[2]

[1] Integration College, Yanbian University, Yanbian, China
2021010828@ybu.edu.cn
[2] Institute of Intelligent Information Processing, Yanbian University, Yanbian, China
yhzhao@ybu.edu.cn
[3] Foreign Language College, Yanbian University, Yanbian, China

Abstract. Currently, the mainstream approach for Korean-Chinese machine translation is to improve the performance of translation models by building upon existing deep learning models. However, there has been insufficient focus on leveraging the linguistic relationship between Korean and Chinese to enhance translation quality. This paper proposes an improvement method that uses the natural connection between the two languages-the Sino-Korean words. Firstly, we shorten the word vector distance of the Sino-Korean words in the semantic space to extract the independent language features of the Sino-Korean words. Secondly, we propose a fine-tuning model to solve mistranslation and translation ambiguity issues caused by 1:N Sino-Korean word pairs. Lastly, we add the coverage loss function to the machine translation model to reduce duplication of translation. This paper conducted experiments on the datasets SWRC and East Asia Daily. Compared with the baseline model, the score of Chinese-to-Korean translation on the SWRC and the East Asia Daily increased by 6.41 BLEU points and 4.09 BLEU points respectively; and the score of Korean-to-Chinese translation increased by 8.43 BLEU points and 4.13 BLEU points respectively.

Keywords: Machine translation · Word Embedding Alignment · Ambiguity · Loss of Coverage

1 Introduction

The Korean ethnic group is one of the minority ethnic groups in China. Korean-Chinese machine translation plays a pivotal role in facilitating cultural exchange between the two nationalities. Machine Translation (MT) [15] is the task of translating a text from one language to another using a computer program. MT has progressed through three distinct stages: Rule-based machine translation(RBMT) [11], Statistical machine translation (SMT) [16], and Neural

Y. Feng and C. Feng (Eds.): CCMT 2023, CCIS 1922, pp. 37–49, 2023.
https://doi.org/10.1007/978-981-99-7894-6_4

Machine Translation (NMT) [2]. The two previous methods have respective issues of high translation costs and low quality of generated translations, which result in less-than-ideal translation outcomes [14]. NMT has shown significant improvements in machine translation. Therefore, NMT has become the mainstream approach. and it mainly includes Recurrent Neural Networks (RNN) [3], Sequence-to-Sequence Model [7], and Transformer [18].

Most research focuses primarily on model innovation because NMT has shown significant improvements in translation quality. But they weren't concerned the natural connections between languages. Although Chinese and Korean do not belong to the same language family, there are natural connections –the Sino words [8]. The Sino words refer to the vocabulary derived from Classical Chinese that exists in languages spoken in countries within the Chinese cultural sphere. Due to language evolution and cultural development, the Sino-Korean words exist in a 1:N phenomenon which means that a single Korean word may correspond to multiple Chinese words. The polysemy of these words often leads to translation errors and confusion during the machine translation process.

To address the aforementioned drawbacks, we propose a Korean-Chinese bilingual machine translation model that uses Sino-Korean words and a coverage loss function. Firstly, we enhance the semantic correspondence between Sino-Korean words in the semantic space. We propose a fine-tuning process to refine the independent language feature vectors of the 1:N Sino-Korea word pairs, reducing ambiguities caused by such pairs. Secondly, we introduce a coverage loss function [6,17] that encourages the model to focus on unseen words, reducing the occurrence of translation repetitions. Finally, we evaluate the performance of our model on both the SWRC dataset and the East Asian Daily dataset. The experimental results provide compelling evidence for the effectiveness of our model in bilingual translation between Korean and Chinese.

We can summarize our contributions as follows:

- We propose a Korean-Chinese machine translation model based on independent language features and coverage loss.
- We introduce Sino-Korean words into the Korean-Chinese machine translation task. Besides we propose a fine-tuning model for balancing the position of the Sino-Korean word pairs in semantic space.
- We assess the performance of our model using two distinct datasets and confirm its efficacy through validation.

2   Related Work

2.1   Korean-to-Chinese Machine Translation

With the advancement of machine translation, Korean-to-Chinese machine translation has witnessed significant progress. In 2019, Park et al. [13] presented the HH-Conv-Transformer model, a Korean-to-Chinese machine translation approach that used Sino-Korean words as anchors. This model replaced Sino-Korean words with corresponding Chinese vocabulary as the input for machine translation. An illustration of this approach is provided in Table 1.

Table 1. Examples of Sino-Korean

Systems	Sentences
Korean	명령은 아래와 같이 반포되었다.
HH-Convert	命令은 아래와 같이 颁布 되었다.
Chinese	命令颁布如下。
Korean	양국은 광범한 영역에서의 공동 이익을 확인했다。
HH-Convert	两国은 广范한 领域에서의 共同 利益을 确认했다。
Chinese	两国在广泛的领域确认了共同利益。

2.2 Multilingual Unsupervised and Supervised Embeddings

In the field of word vector alignment, Facebook introduced the Multilingual Unsupervised or Supervised word Embeddings (MUSE) [5], which facilitates the alignment of word vectors between arbitrary bilingual pairs. In 2019, Xilun Chen [4] extended the MUSE framework to develop a multilingual version of the MUSE model. This enhanced model allows for multiple source languages to be inputted along with a target language.

The extended MUSE model consists of encoders, decoders, and discriminators [9]. The source languages and the target language are mapped to the shared embedding space using separate encoders. The vectors in this space can be generated into language-specific word vectors using the corresponding decoder. The vectors generated by the decoder can then be distinguished by a discriminator, which determines whether the vector is derived from authentic target language word vectors or obtained through conversion from the source language.

3 Method

3.1 Independent Language Feature Extraction Model

The aim of this study is to enhance machine translation accuracy by using the Sino-Korean word pairs. We train an independent language feature extraction model using a Korean-Chinese-English multilingual dictionary and the Sino-Korean word pairs. We acquire the independent language features of the Sino-Korean word pairs by this model. And we introduce a fine-tuning model to readjust the relative position of 1:N word pairs in semantic space. Finally, we replace the initial word vectors in the translation model with the independent language feature of the Sino-Korean word pairs to improve the performance of the translation model.

We construct a Korean-Chinese bilingual dictionary using an English-Chinese bilingual dictionary and an English-Korean bilingual dictionary, with English as the pivot language. Next, we employ the Hanjaro[1] method to extract the Sino-Korean word pairs from the parallel corpus, which serve as additional word pairs for the Korean-Chinese bilingual dictionary mentioned earlier. Finally, we use

---

[1] The tool can be found at http://hanjaro.juntong.or.kr/.

the constructed dictionary as anchor points in the extended MUSE model to extract independent language features for the Sino-Korean word pairs.

Antonios Anastasopoulos [1] pointed out that in bilingual or multilingual settings, a prominent pivot language is often not the source or target language. Furthermore, when there are significant differences between the source and target languages, it is preferable to select multiple languages to strengthen the correspondence of word vectors. Therefore, we select Korean, Chinese, and English as the pivot languages for mapping. We choose one of these languages as the target language and the others as the source language input to the extended MUSE model. Through multiple iterations of the model, we achieve word vector alignment and select the word vectors in the shared embedding space as the independent language features of each language.

Due to the aforementioned strategy, which alters the positions of the Sino-Korean word pairs in the semantic space. It is possible to create an imbalance in the positions of 1:N the Sino-Korean word pairs in the semantic space. This imbalance could lead to phenomena such as mistranslation and translation confusion during the translation process, thereby diminishing the effectiveness of machine translation. Specific examples of mistranslation and translation confusion are presented in Table 2.

Table 2. Examples of wrong and confusing translation

	Mistranslation	Translation confusion
Korean word	공포	의장
Corresponding Chinese word	['恐惧', '恐怖', '公布']	['主席', '议长']
Target sentence	审讯日期将要公布.	他将辞去议长之职.
Generated sentence	审讯日期将由恐惧.	他将辞去主席的职责.

To validate the aforementioned idea, we use cosine distance to measure the proximity of 1:N Sino-Korean word pairs in the semantic space. Through calculations, it is observed that when the Chinese words of the 1:N word pairs are synonymous, the cosine distance between Chinese synonymous words may be smaller than the cosine distance between Korean words and Chinese words. As shown in Fig. 1(A). (의장 主席 议长) is a Sino-Korean word pair, and the distance "c" between " 主席 " and " 议长 " is smaller than the distance "a" between " 主席 " and " 의장 and also is smaller than the distance "b" between " 议长 " and " 의장 " respectively. When the Chinese word pairs do not have a synonymous relationship, it is possible that the distance between a specific Chinese word and a Korean word is much smaller or larger than the distance between the other Chinese words and the Korean word. As shown in Fig. 1(C) the distance "a" between the Chinese word " 市场 " and the Korean word " 시상 " is significantly smaller compared to the distance "b" between the Chinese word " 市长 " and the Korean word " 시상 ". Therefore, the occurrence of mistranslation and translation ambiguity in Korean-to-Chinese machine translation may be attributed to the uneven distances.

To address the aforementioned issues, we propose a fine-tuning model. The objective of this model is to adjust the positions of the 1:N Sino-Korean word pairs in the semantic space to achieve a more balanced distribution and enhance the accuracy of Korean-to-Chinese translation.

Mikolov et al. [10] demonstrated that there is a strong linear correlation between vector spaces of two languages. Xing et al. [19] further showed that enforcing linear mapping as an orthogonal matrix can achieve higher performance. Inspired by these findings, our method introduces two orthogonal matrices as linear layers to map the word vectors of the Sino-Korean word pairs. This mapping aims to equalize the distances between the mapped Chinese words and Korean vocabulary, thereby reducing translation errors caused by uneven cosine distances between the 1:N Sino-Korean word pairs. Specifically, as shown in Fig. 1(A) and Fig. 1(B), Fig. 1(A) illustrates the relative positions of (의장 主 席 议长) before fine-tuning, while Fig. 1(B) depicts their relative positions after fine-tuning. It can be observed that after fine-tuning, the distances between these three terms in the semantic space become more balanced. This indicates the effectiveness of the fine-tuning model. Furthermore, to reduce the issue of translation confusion caused by close distances between Chinese words of the 1:N Sino-Korean word pairs, the fine-tuning model should also ensure that the distances between the mapped Chinese words exceed a certain threshold. This can be observed in Fig. 1(C) and Fig. 1(D): Fig. 1(C) represents the relative positions of (시상 市场 市长) before fine-tuning, while Fig. 1(D) depicts their relative positions after fine-tuning. It is evident that after fine-tuning, the distances between these three terms in the semantic space are more balanced.

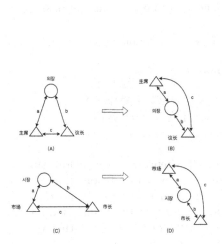

Fig. 1. Examples

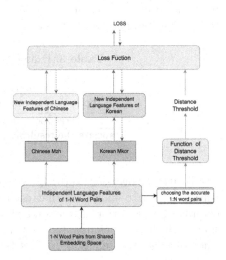

Fig. 2. Fine-Tuning Model. Chinese Mzh is the linear layer for Chinese; Korean Mkor is the linear layer for Korean; LOSS is loss value

the specific process is shown in Eq. 1 and Eq. 2:

$$Loss = \sum_{i=1}^{N} (a_i + |a_i - a_1|) + \sum_{j=1}^{m} max(0, (s - b_j))$$ (1)

$$s = \frac{1}{h * h'} \sum_{i=1}^{h} \sum_{j=1}^{h'} a_{ij}, \text{vocab} = \{w_1, w_2, \cdots, w_h\}$$ (2)

where a_i is the cosine distance between the Korean word and the Chinese words in the 1:N Sino-Korean word pairs, b_j is the cosine distance between Chinese words in the 1:N Sino-Korean word pairs, s is the shortest distance between multiple Chinese words corresponding to a Korean word, $vocab$ is the set of 1:N Sino-Korean word pairs that can be translated correctly, w is a Sino-Korean word pair, h is the length of the set $vocab$, h' is the number of Chinese words corresponding to a w. The specific model diagram is shown in Fig. 2

3.2 Translation Model

Due to the poor quality of the training data corpus in this study, there is a lack of alignment between the source language and the target language. As a result, during the experimental process, we observed the issue of repeated translations in the generated output, as illustrated in Table 3. To address this problem, we propose the introduction of a coverage loss function [6,17], aiming to mitigate the occurrence of repeated translations. The coverage loss function is derived from the coverage mechanism for generating text summaries, which can prevent the model from generating repetitive sequences and missing translations.

Table 3. Examples of repeat translation

Repetitive translation	
Input Korean sentence	메리 크리스마스!
Target sentence	祝你耶诞节快乐!
Translate the resulting sentences	祝你圣诞节圣诞节!

We use a coverage vector c^t to record all attention scores before time t, which is used to judge whether each token has appeared before time t. The coverage loss function is the sum of the minimum values of a^t and c^t at all times, which is a penalty item for the loss function of the translation model. The coverage loss function enables the model to focus on words that do not appear, thereby reducing the phenomenon of repeated translations. The final loss function consists of two parts: translation loss and coverage loss, as shown in Eq. 3, Eq. 4 and Eq. 5:

$$c^t = \sum_{t'=1}^{t-1} a^{t'}$$ (3)

$$\text{coverloss}_t = \sum_i \min(a_i^t, c_i^t) \tag{4}$$

$$Loss = Loss_{translate} + \text{coverloss} \tag{5}$$

where a^t is the joint attention of the last layer of the decoder at time step t.

Based on the above information, we propose the machine translation model in this paper, known as HH-Cover-Transformer, which based on independent linguistic features and coverage loss, as illustrated in Fig. 3.

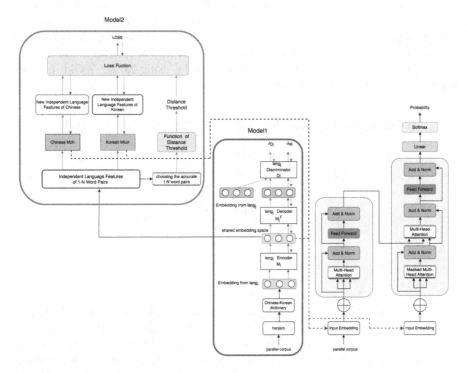

Fig. 3. HH-Cover-Transformer. In model1, the encoder and decoder are orthogonal matrices, J_{D_j} represents the loss value of the discriminator D_j, and J_{M_i} represents the loss value of the source language encoder.

In the experimental process, we first obtain the independent language features of the Sino-Korean word pairs through Model 1. Then, we refine the positions of the 1:N Sino-Korean word pairs in the semantic space using Model 2. Finally, we use the final independent language features of the Sino-Korean word pairs as the corresponding word vectors, which are then fed into the Transformer model.

4   Experiment

4.1   Datasets

This paper uses the Korean-Chinese public dataset the SWRC and the East Asia Daily, which are divided into the training set, verification set, and test set. The specific scale is shown in Table 4.

Each data entry in the dataset consists of a Chinese sentence and its corresponding Korean sentence. Park et al. [12] experimentally verified that subword segmentation performs optimally in English-Korean machine translation. Therefore, we adopt a subword segmentation approach. For Chinese texts, we first use jieba to segment the middle sentence, and then use SentencePiece to realize the second word segmentation of the segmented sentences. For Korean texts, the sentences are initially segmented into word-level nodes using Konlpy's Okt method, followed by a similar subword segmentation process.

Table 4. The statistical descriptions of SWRC and East Asia Daily

	SWRC	East Asia Daily
Training set	51294	150756
Validation set	2000	4811
Test set	2000	4812

4.2   Settings

The experiments for extracting language-independent features are conducted on a hardware setup comprising an RTX5000 graphics card and 16G video memory. The operating system is Ubuntu 20.04, with Python 3.7 as the development language and Pytorch 1.8 as the deep-learning framework. The language-independent feature extraction model uses the 300-dimensional Wiki word vectors in fastText as the input of the initial word vectors and uses the English-Chinese and English-Korean bilingual dictionaries collated by Facebook to build the initial Korean-Chinese bilingual dictionary.

4.3   Main Results

We compare the experimental results of a machine translation model based on independent language features and coverage loss (HH-Cover-Transformer) on the SWRC dataset and the East Asia Daily dataset with other public methods. The results are shown in Table 5. It can be seen from Table 5 that our method in this paper has 51.65 BLEU points for Chinese-to-Korean translation and 51.23 BLEU points for Korean-to-Chinese translation on the SWRC dataset of the same scale (only the first 284 pieces of data of test set are translated due to equipment and time problems). On the East Asia Daily dataset, our method has 37.90 BLEU points for Chinese-to-Korean translation and 35.47 BLEU points for Korean-to-Chinese translation. Both of them have achieved good results.

Table 5. Results of comparative experiments

Model	Chinese-to-Korean(BLEU)		Korean-to-Chinese(BLEU)	
	SWRC _Test	East Asia Daily_Test	SWRC _Test	East Asia Daily_Test
Seq2Seq	16.85	21.88	8.24	12.97
Transformer	45.24	33.81	42.80	31.34
HH-Conv-Transformer	49.17	34.43	49.58	33.9
HH-Cover-Transformer	**51.65**	**37.90**	**51.23**	**35.47**

Our model adds a coverage loss function to the baseline model, which alleviates the problem of repeated sequences. And we shorten the distance between Sino-Korean word pairs in the semantic space. Compared with the use of Sino-Korean character pairs, the method in this paper uses the semantic relationship of Sino-Korean word pairs at a deeper level. Therefore, compared with the Transformer model and the HH-Conv-Transformer model, in Chinese-to-Korean translation, the score has increased by 6.41 BLEU points and 2.48 BLEU points respectively on the SWRC and the score has increased by 4.09 BLEU points and 3.47 BLEU points respectively on the East Asia Daily. Compared with the Transformer model and the HH-Conv-Transformer model, in Korean-to-Chinese the score of translation has increased by 8.43 BLEU points and 1.65 BLEU points respectively on SWRC and the score has increased by 4.13 BLEU points and 1.54 BLEU points respectively on the East Asia Daily.

5 Analysis

5.1 Ablation Experiments

In order to explore the role of each module, this paper conducts ablation experiments on the SWRC dataset and East Asia Daily dataset. The experimental results are shown in Table 6.

1to1-Transformer is the transformer that is added to the 1:1 Sino-Korean word pairs. 1to1-1toNN-Transformer is the transformer that adds the 1:1 word pairs and the 1:N word pairs without fine-tuning. 1to1-1toN-Transformer is the transformer that uses the 1:1 word pairs and the 1:N word pairs with fine-tuning. 1to1-Cover-Transformer is a transformer adds 1:1 Sino-Korean word pairs and the coverage function. CKT stands for Chinese-to-Korean Translation. KCT stands for Korean-to-Chinese Translation.

- In order to verify the effectiveness of the independent feature extraction, 1to1-Transformer in CKT the improvement over the baseline model for the two datasets is 2.70 and 1.66 respectively. It is over the baseline model for the two datasets is 1.8 and 1.32 in KCT.

Table 6. Results of ablation experiments

Model	Chinese-to-Korean(BLEU)		Korean-to-Chinese(BLEU)	
	SWRC _Test	East Asia Daily_Test	SWRC _Test	East Asia Daily_Test
Transformer	45.24	33.81	42.80	31.34
1to1-Transformer	47.94	35.47	44.60	33.66
1to1-1toNN-Transformer	–	–	41.83	28.58
1to1-1toN-Transformer	–	–	45.70	33.94
1to1-Cover-Transformer	51.65	37.90	48.04	34.23
HH-Cover-Transformer	**51.65**	**37.90**	**51.23**	**35.47**

- In order to verify the effectiveness of the fine-tuning model, 1to1-1toNN-Transformer is lower than Transformer 0.97 and 2.76 on the two datasets in KCT. What's more, 1to1-1toN-Transformer is higher than Transformer 2.90, 2.60 and is higher than 1to1-Transformer 1.10, 0.28 on the two datasets in KCT.
- In order to verify the effectiveness of the coverage loss function, 1to1-Cover-Transformer is higher than 1to1-Transformer 3.71 and 2.43 on the two datasets in CKT. And it also is higher 1to1-Transformer 3.44 and 0.57 in KCT.

5.2   Case Study

Visualization of the Independent Language Features. In Sect. 2.1, we performed the alignment of Chinese word pairs in the semantic space. In this section, we will present a comparison of 10 selected Chinese word pairs to illustrate this alignment. The specific details are shown in Fig. 4.

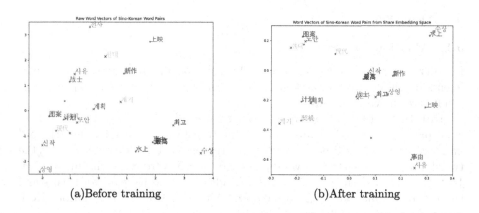

(a)Before training   (b)After training

Fig. 4. Comparison of word vectors.

Figure 4(a) presents the initial word vector visualization of the 10 selected Chinese word pairs. On the other hand, Fig. 4(b) displays the independent language features of the same 10 Chinese word pairs after training. The visual comparison between Fig. 4(a) and 4(b) confirms the effectiveness of our word vector alignment work. It demonstrates the role of our independent feature extraction model in aligning the vectors and reinforces the strengthened correspondence of the Sino-Korean word pairs in the semantic space.

Results of the Fine-Tuning Model. In Sect. 2.1, we propose a fine-tuning model to solve the issue of imbalanced semantic distribution in 1:N Sino-Korean word pairs. In this section, we will present the changes in cosine distances within the semantic space for 1:N Sino-Korean word pairs The specific details are presented in Table 7.

Table 7. The changes in cosine distances

Kor-Zh imbalanced distribution		
Before Fine-tuning		
kor-zh1	kor-zh2	zh1-zh2
(사고 思考 事故)　　**0.3308**	0.8765	0.7513
(생산 产生 生产)　　**0.2910**	0.8493	0.6321
After Fine-tuning		
kor-zh1	kor-zh2	zh1-zh2
(사고 思考 事故)　　0.2060	0.2185	0.7583
(생산 产生 生产)　　0.2157	0.2104	0.7608
Zh-Zh distribution proximity		
Before Fine-tuning		
kor-zh1	kor-zh2	zh1-zh2
(관계 关系 联系)　　0.3578	0.5562	**0.2564**
(수집 搜集 收集)　　0.4264	0.4534	**0.1759**
After Fine-tuning		
kor-zh1	kor-zh2	zh1-zh2
(관계 关系 联系)　　0.2088	0.2167	0.7597
(수집 搜集 收集)　　0.2170	0.2084	0.7592

Table 7 comprises two sections: 1:N Sino-Korean word pairs with imbalanced distances between Korean and Chinese vocabulary and 1:N Sino-Korean word pairs with excessively close distances between Chinese vocabulary. "kor-zh1" represents the cosine distance between the Korean vocabulary and the first Chinese vocabulary in the 1:N Sino-Korean word pairs. "kor-zh2" represents the cosine distance between the Korean vocabulary and the second Chinese vocabulary. "zh1-zh2" represents the cosine distance between the two Chinese vocabularies.

Translation Examples. In this section, we primarily showcase the translation results of the same test sentence using different translation models, as presented in Table 8. The color red indicates mistranslations in the translated sentences, including translation errors, omissions, and additions. Underlining denotes instances of repetitive translations within the translated sentences.

Table 8. Translation examples generated by different models

	Chinese-to-Korean	Korean-to-Chine
Source sentence	她深深地叹息	그는 야구를하고 있다
Reference sentence	그녀는 깊이 탄식 했다.	他在打棒球 .
SeqtoSeq	그들은 의기투합한다.	他在棒球棒球 .
Transformer	그녀는 깊이 탄식 하는 것을 깊이 당했다.	他在棒球棒球 .
HH-Conv-Transformer	그녀는 깊이 쉬 었 다 .	他正在打棒球 .
Our Model	그녀는 깊이 탄식 했다.	他在打棒球 .

6   Conclusion

This study aims to enhance the accuracy of Korean-Chinese machine translation by using the inherent linguistic connections between the two languages. Firstly, we employ Hanjaro approach to extract Sino-Korean words from the parallel corpus. Next, we use word embedding alignment techniques to strengthen the semantic correspondence of the Sino-Korean word pairs. And we propose a fine-tuning model to address the issue of polysemy in the Sino-Korean words and reduce translation errors caused by uneven distribution of distances. Finally, we introduce a coverage loss function to mitigate the problem of repetitive translations in the translation results,. Extensive experimental results and analyses demonstrate significant improvements achieved by our system. In the future, we plan to incorporate more language rules into the field of machine translation to further enhance its capabilities.

Acknowledgement. This work is supported by Major program of the National Social Science Foundation of China [grant numbers 22&ZD305], National Natural Science Foundation of China [grant numbers 62162062]. Jilin Provincial Department of Science and Technology Development Plan Project [grant numbers: 20220203127SF], State Language Commission of China under Grant No.YB135-76. Scientific research project for building world top discipline of Foreign Languages and Literatures of Yanbian University under Grant No. 18YLPY13. The school-enterprise cooperation project of Yanbian University [2020-15].

References

1. Anastasopoulos, A., Neubig, G.: Should all cross-lingual embeddings speak english? arXiv preprint arXiv:1911.03058 (2019)
2. Bansal, Y., et al.: Data scaling laws in NMT: the effect of noise and architecture. In: International Conference on Machine Learning, pp. 1466–1482. PMLR (2022)

3. Bensalah, N., Ayad, H., Adib, A., Ibn El Farouk, A.: CRAN: an hybrid CNN-RNN attention-based model for Arabic machine translation. In: Ben Ahmed, M., Teodorescu, H.-N.L., Mazri, T., Subashini, P., Boudhir, A.A. (eds.) Networking, Intelligent Systems and Security. SIST, vol. 237, pp. 87–102. Springer, Singapore (2022). https://doi.org/10.1007/978-981-16-3637-0_7

4. Chen, X., Cardie, C.: Unsupervised multilingual word embeddings. arXiv preprint arXiv:1808.08933 (2018)

5. Conneau, A., Lample, G., Ranzato, M., Denoyer, L., Jégou, H.: Word translation without parallel data. arXiv preprint arXiv:1710.04087 (2017)

6. Deaton, J., Jacobs, A., Kenealy, K., See, A.: Transformers and pointer-generator networks for abstractive summarization (2019)

7. Gong, S., Li, M., Feng, J., Wu, Z., Kong, L.: Diffuseq: sequence to sequence text generation with diffusion models. arXiv preprint arXiv:2210.08933 (2022)

8. Ito, C., Feldman, N.H.: Iterated learning models of language change: a case study of sino-korean accent. Cogn. Sci. **46**(4), e13115 (2022)

9. Kusner, M.J., Hernández-Lobato, J.M.: Gans for sequences of discrete elements with the gumbel-softmax distribution. arXiv preprint arXiv:1611.04051 (2016)

10. Mikolov, T., Le, Q.V., Sutskever, I.: Exploiting similarities among languages for machine translation. arXiv preprint arXiv:1309.4168 (2013)

11. Mondal, S.K., Zhang, H., Kabir, H.D., Ni, K., Dai, H.N.: Machine translation and its evaluation: a study. Artif. Intell. Rev., 1–90 (2023)

12. Park, D., Jang, Y., Kim, H.: Korean-English machine translation with multiple tokenization strategy. arXiv preprint arXiv:2105.14274 (2021)

13. Park, J., Zhao, H.: Korean-to-Chinese machine translation using Chinese character as pivot clue. arXiv preprint arXiv:1911.11008 (2019)

14. Ranathunga, S., Lee, E.S.A., Skenduli, M.P., Shekhar, R., Alam, M., Kaur, R.: Neural machine translation for low-resource languages: a survey. ACM Comput. Surv. **55**(11), 1–37 (2023)

15. Raulji, J.K., Saini, J.R., Pal, K., Kotecha, K.: A novel framework for Sanskrit-Gujarati symbolic machine translation system. Int. J. Adv. Comput. Sci. Appl. **13**(4), 374–380 (2022)

16. Sebastian, M.P.: Malayalam natural language processing: challenges in building a phrase-based statistical machine translation system. ACM Trans. Asian Low-Res. Lang. Inf. Process. **22**(4), 1–51 (2023)

17. See, A., Liu, P.J., Manning, C.D.: Get to the point: summarization with pointer-generator networks. arXiv preprint arXiv:1704.04368 (2017)

18. Vaswani, A., et al.: Attention is all you need. Adv. Neural Inf. Process. Syst. **30** (2017)

19. Xing, C., Wang, D., Liu, C., Lin, Y.: Normalized word embedding and orthogonal transform for bilingual word translation. In: Proceedings of the 2015 Conference of the North American Chapter of the Association for Computational Linguistics: Human Language Technologies, pp. 1006–1011 (2015)

NJUNLP's Submission for CCMT 2023 Quality Estimation Task

Zhejian Lai, Xiang Geng, Yu Zhang, Jiajun Chen, and Shujian Huang[✉]

National Key Laboratory for Novel Software Technology,
Nanjing University, Nanjing, China
{laizj,gx,zhangy}@smail.nju.edu.cn, {chenjj,huangsj}@nju.edu.cn

Abstract. Quality Estimation is a task aiming to estimate the quality of translations without relying on any references. This paper describes our submission for CCMT 2023 quality estimation sentence-level task for English-to-Chinese (EN-ZH). Due to the challenges of costly annotations and small dataset sizes in the QE field, many researchers have attempted to leverage rich parallel corpora for unsupervised learning through methods such as uncertainty quantification, and data augmentation. Existing mainstream unsupervised QE methods exhibit good diversity and variability, so we test these methods individually as well as their ensemble effect.

Keywords: Quality Estimation · Unsupervised Learning

1 Introduction

Machine translation (MT) quality estimation (QE) is a crucial task to estimate the quality of MT outputs when reference translations are unavailable [13]. QE has a wide range of downstream applications. It can provide precise guidance for post-editing processes and serve as a confidence metric for online translation systems.

Supervised QE refers to the approach where the model has access to additional QE resources during the training process. On the other hand, unsupervised QE can only utilize monolingual and parallel corpora for training. Therefore, the emergence of unsupervised QE reduces the model's reliance on expensive and scarce annotated QE data, leading to extensive discussions among researchers. Traditional QE methods are the pioneers of supervised QE, as they leverage manual features which are time-consuming and expensive to get to accomplish the task. [6]. Later, researchers try to generate automatic neural features by applying neural networks [1,11]. However, there are still serious problems as to the fact that QE data is scarce which limits the improvement of QE models. The Predictor-Estimator framework proposed by Kim et al. [5] is devoted to addressing this problem, and under this framework, bilingual knowledge can be transferred from parallel data to QE tasks. However, the Estimator requires annotated data to establish a connection with real-world QE data, whereas unsupervised

© The Author(s), under exclusive license to Springer Nature Singapore Pte Ltd. 2023
Y. Feng and C. Feng (Eds.): CCMT 2023, CCIS 1922, pp. 50–56, 2023.
https://doi.org/10.1007/978-981-99-7894-6_5

QE does not require it. The following are some mainstream unsupervised QE methods: Cui et al. (2021) [3] implement a masking technique where reference tokens are randomly selected and replaced with tokens sampled from the translation language model (TLM) [2] generation probability distribution. Tuan et al. [14] directly generate pseudo MTs using a neural machine translation (NMT) model and obtain labels by matching these MTs with corresponding references. Both of these methods belong to the category of data augmentation techniques. Nowadays, Zheng et al. [15] propose SSQE that shows the conditional probability computed by the cross-lingual masked language model (CMLM) is a good indicator of translation quality. It successfully links the uncertainty associated with token restoration to its corresponding quality label. We believe the above methods that have not been fine-tuned with real QE data has good complementarity. The ensemble of them can achieve excellent results in unsupervised experiments.

This paper introduces our sentence-level quality estimation submission for CCMT 2023 in detail. Our main focus is on unsupervised systems, and we have submitted the results of integrating state-of-the-art unsupervised Quality Estimation (QE) models. Eventually, a basic averaging ensemble and neural ensemble are used to get a better result. These results are expected to establish a bridge to real-world data once QE data is introduced, thereby further enhancing our capabilities. To provide a comparison, we also fine-tune it using QE data, resulting in the submitted supervised system.

2   Methods

2.1   Unsupervised Methods

DirectQE. The DirectQE [3] framework consists of two main components: the generator and the detector. The generator is trained on parallel data to generate pseudo QE data, while the detector can be pre-trained and fine-tuned using both the pseudo data and real QE data, with the same objective in mind.

In the DirectQE framework, the generator is trained using a masked language model that is conditioned on the source text, denoted as X. During the training process, for each parallel pair of source text X and corresponding translation Y, DirectQE randomly masks 15% of the tokens in Y and attempts to recover them. The masked tokens are then predicted by DirectQE using sampling strategies based on the generated probabilities during the pseudo data generation procedure. The annotation strategy used is straightforward: if a generated token differs from the original token, it is annotated as 'BAD', and the sentence-level score is calculated as the ratio of 'BAD' tokens in the sentence.

The detector performs joint predictions of word-level tags and sentence-level scores. It first undergoes pre-training on the pseudo QE data and then fine-tuning on the real QE data, while maintaining the same training objective throughout the process.

NMT+TER. Tuan et al. [14] generate candidate translations for source sentences using two different methods. Firstly, they employ the NMT model to translate each source sentence, resulting in one form of translation. Then, they treat the target sentences as pseudo post-edits and apply the TER tools [12] to examine the insertions, deletions, and substitutions between the reference translations and the generated translations to identify errors in each candidate translation.

SSQE. The fundamental steps of SSQE [15] involves masking certain target words within the machine-translated sentence and then utilizing a CMLM to reconstruct the masked target words depending on the source sentence and the observed target words. As Monte-Carlo Dropout [4] is proven conducive to the performance of unsupervised QE models, SSQE employs this method to perform multiple inferences on each token, resulting in a significant improvement in overall performance. In simple terms, a target word is deemed accurate if it can be successfully reconstructed based on its contextual cues. By evaluating the successful recovery probability of target words, the translation quality is estimated. The higher the probability, the easier it is for the word to be considered 'OK'. Eventually, the word-level predictions are summarized to derive the sentence-level quality score (Fig. 1).

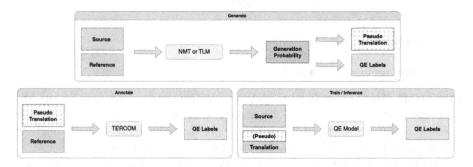

Fig. 1. The modules utilized by the three unsupervised methods. In the SSQE model, labels are derived through a comparative analysis of generation probabilities against a predefined threshold. Conversely, the remaining two approaches generate pseudo-translations and subsequently autonomously annotate them, thereby training the model to directly predict labels.

2.2 Supervised Methods

We perform fine-tuning on all the unsupervised models mentioned above using authentic QE data, which are extensively trained in an unsupervised environment.

3   Experiments

In this section, we will provide a comprehensive overview of our experiments. This will include detailed information about the dataset used, the hyperparameters employed, and the performance of individual models, among other aspects.

3.1   Dataset

QE Dataset. Our participation focuses on the English-to-Chinese language direction, which 1,528 development data instances (DEV). Please note that we do not use the training set from the QE dataset provided by CCMT2023. In our final submission of the supervised system and the baseline model, we incorporate the QE task data from WMT2020.

Parallel Dataset. To pre-train the XLM-R model, we convert parallel data into pseudo data in the form of QE triplets. Out of the total 20,305,269 parallel sentences from the WMT 2020 QE task, we utilize an additional 500,000 sentences. It is important to note that we do not utilize the parallel data provided by the CCMT QE task.

3.2   Settings

Metrics. The main metric of the quality estimation sentence-level task is Pearson's Correlation Coefficient. Mean Absolute Error (MAE) and Root Mean Squared Error (RMSE) will be considered as metrics as well.

Hyper-parameters. The transformer-based generator employed a mask ratio of 45% and achieved an average HTER score of approximately 16%–18% for the pseudo data. Apart from these modifications, all other sets remained consistent with the original DirectQE model. The NMT-based generator utilized a learning rate scheduler that adjusted the training learning rate using an inverse square root function. As for the detector component, the XLM-R-large model was employed, and all parameters associated with it were updated accordingly. For NMT+TER and SSQE, we follow the setting of hyper-parameters under the description provided in their corresponding published papers.

Tokenize. We first use jieba[1] to tokenize the Chinese dataset. In the step of the generator, we use BPE [10] to tokenize both the source and target sentences, while in the step of detector SentencePiece [8] is used to tokenize the sentences for XLM-R model. The step of BPE is set to 30,000, and we use all tokens after tokenization. Regarding the QE DEV set of CCMT 2023, we utilized pkuseg [9] for Chinese translation segmentation and employed the SentencePiece for tokenization.

---

[1] https://github.com/fxsjy/jieba.

3.3   Single Model Results

Our baseline model is a supervised XLMRQE, which simply utilizes the XLMR-Large architecture to directly predict the final HTER score by pooling the hidden layer outputs of each token. The results of single models are shown in Table 1.

Table 1. Single model results of the CCMT 2023 on DEV set.The results have been magnified by a factor of 100.

method	Pearson	MAE	RMSE
XLMR	20.55	43.07	44.62
SSQE	17.91	40.93	43.79
DirectQE	**21.13**	**19.33**	**21.65**
NMT+TER	16.62	46.13	48.44

It can be observed that DirectQE surpasses the baseline model without fine-tuning using real QE data, highlighting the superiority of the DirectQE method in an unsupervised environment. On the other hand, NMT+TER, which is also a data augmentation method, exhibits poorer performance.

3.4   Ensemble

We experiment with two distinct ensemble methods at the sentence level. The first method is the averaging ensemble, which involves averaging the results obtained from the model outputs. The second method, referred to as the neural ensemble, involves collecting the Human Translation Error Rate (HTER) values from the training and development datasets of all the aforementioned models. Then we trained a simple neural network model to learn and utilize these HTER values for predicting the desired golden HTER values.

The ensemble results are shown in Table 2, and we can see that the neural ensemble result slightly outperforms the other one at the sentence level. The results of the two-model ensemble indicate a significant difference between NMT+TER and DirectQE, resulting in individual improvements of +5.40/+0.89 Pearson score for the two original models, while the inclusion of SSQE only leads to a marginal increase of +0.30 Pearson score in the final outcome. The importance of model diversity in ensemble learning has been widely recognized [7]. Consequently, this observation underscores the existence of substantial conceptual distinctions between DirectQE and NMT+TER. Meanwhile, their integration almost encompasses the capabilities of SSQE. The ensemble of NMT+TER and SSQE simultaneously resulted in an individual improvement of +1.36/+2.65 Pearson score, indicating that there is also the considerable disparity between SSQE and NMT+TER.

In our empirical analysis, it becomes evident that a single DirectQE model consistently outperforms the two-model averaging ensemble in which it is included. This observation implies that the average ensemble approach equally distributes weights across all constituent models, leading to suboptimal performance due to the varying capabilities of the models involved. To elucidate further, it is noteworthy that DirectQE consistently exhibits outstanding performance, whereas the incorporation of other models introduces aspects of inconsistency and interference, ultimately diminishing the overall effectiveness of the decision-making process. The result of neural ensemble methods surpassing the individual performance of the DirectQE model serves as empirical validation for this assertion.

Table 2. Ensemble model results of the CCMT 2023 on DEV set. The results have been magnified by a factor of 100.

ensemble	Average			Neural		
	Pearson	MAE	RMSE	Pearson	MAE	RMSE
DirectQE & NMT+TER	20.57	32.38	34.34	22.02	24.29	26.33
SSQE & DirectQE	20.73	29.82	32.11	21.89	**23.13**	**25.32**
SSQE & NMT+TER	19.25	43.50	45.74	19.27	43.24	45.51
SSQE & DirectQE & NMT+TER	20.99	35.17	37.23	**22.29**	23.97	26.04

4   Conclusion

This paper presents our submissions for the sentence-level task of Quality Estimation at CCMT 2023. We develope our systems using mainstream unsupervised QE techniques, utilizing the NJUQE[2] framework and Transformers package. To investigate their varying performance, we employe both average-based and neural-based methods for integration. Our findings reveal substantial disparities among DirectQE, NMT+TER and SSQE approaches. Furthermore, in our final submission, we include a refined version achieved through integrated unsupervised QE fine-tuning.

References

1. Chen, Z., et al.: Improving machine translation quality estimation with neural network features. In: Proceedings of the Second Conference on Machine Translation, pp. 551–555 (2017)

---

[2] https://github.com/NJUNLP/njuqe.

2. Conneau, A., Lample, G.: Cross-lingual language model pretraining. In: Advances in Neural Information Processing Systems, vol. 32 (2019)
3. Cui, Q., et la.: Directqe: direct pretraining for machine translation quality estimation. In: Proceedings of the AAAI Conference on Artificial Intelligence, vol. 35, pp. 12719–12727 (2021)
4. Gal, Y., Ghahramani, Z.: Dropout as a Bayesian approximation: representing model uncertainty in deep learning. In: International Conference on Machine Learning, pp. 1050–1059. PMLR (2016)
5. Kim, H., Lee, J.H., Na, S.H.: Predictor-estimator using multilevel task learning with stack propagation for neural quality estimation. In: Proceedings of the Second Conference on Machine Translation, pp. 562–568 (2017)
6. Kreutzer, J., Schamoni, S., Riezler, S.: Quality estimation from scratch (quetch): deep learning for word-level translation quality estimation. In: Proceedings of the Tenth Workshop on Statistical Machine Translation, pp. 316–322 (2015)
7. Krogh, A., Vedelsby, J.: Neural network ensembles, cross validation, and active learning. In: Advances in Neural Information Processing Systems, vol. 7 (1994)
8. Kudo, T., Richardson, J.: Sentencepiece: a simple and language independent subword tokenizer and detokenizer for neural text processing. arXiv preprint arXiv:1808.06226 (2018)
9. Luo, R., Xu, J., Zhang, Y., Zhang, Z., Ren, X., Sun, X.: Pkuseg: a toolkit for multi-domain Chinese word segmentation. CoRR abs/1906.11455 (2019), https://arxiv.org/abs/1906.11455
10. Sennrich, R., Haddow, B., Birch, A.: Neural machine translation of rare words with subword units. arXiv preprint arXiv:1508.07909 (2015)
11. Shah, K., Bougares, F., Barrault, L., Specia, L.: Shef-lium-nn: sentence level quality estimation with neural network features. In: Proceedings of the First Conference on Machine Translation: Volume 2, Shared Task Papers, pp. 838–842 (2016)
12. Snover, M., Dorr, B., Schwartz, R., Micciulla, L., Makhoul, J.: A study of translation edit rate with targeted human annotation. In: Proceedings of the 7th Conference of the Association for Machine Translation in the Americas: Technical Papers, pp. 223–231 (2006)
13. Specia, L., Scarton, C., Paetzold, G.H.: Quality estimation for machine translation. Synth. Lect. Hum. Lang. Technol. 11(1), 1–162 (2018)
14. Tuan, Y.L., El-Kishky, A., Renduchintala, A., Chaudhary, V., Guzmán, F., Specia, L.: Quality estimation without human-labeled data. In: Proceedings of the 16th Conference of the European Chapter of the Association for Computational Linguistics: Main Volume, pp. 619–625. Association for Computational Linguistics, April 2021. https://doi.org/10.18653/v1/2021.eacl-main.50, https://aclanthology.org/2021.eacl-main.50
15. Zheng, Y., et al.: Self-supervised quality estimation for machine translation. In: Proceedings of the 2021 Conference on Empirical Methods in Natural Language Processing, pp. 3322–3334 (2021)

HIT-MI&T Lab's Submission to CCMT 2023 Automatic Post-editing Task

Rui Zhang, Jinghao Yuan, Hui Huang, Muyun Yang[✉], and Tiejun Zhao

Research Center on Language Technology,
School of Computer Science and Engineering, Harbin Institute of Technology,
Harbin, China
{23S003048,7203610706,huanghui}@stu.hit.edu.cn,
{yangmuyun,tjzhao}@hit.edu.cn

Abstract. Automatic post-editing (APE) aims to automatically correct the outputs of the machine translation system by learning from manual correction examples. We present the system developed by HIT-MI&T Lab for the CCMT 2023 APE task of Chinese-English direction. We use mBART as the backbone model, and explore different techniques to create synthetic data, including domain selection, forward translation and data augmentation via large language model. Multi-model ensemble is also adopted in our final system. The experiment results on the development set demonstrate the effectiveness of our proposed method.

Keywords: Machine Translation · Automatic Post-Editing · Data Augmentation

1 Introduction

Automatic post-editing as a post-processing procedure for machine translation (MT) aims to correct the outputs of the machine translation system automatically by learning from correction examples. As pointed out by Chatterjee et al. [2], from the application point of view, the APE task is motivated by its possible uses to improve MT output by exploiting information unavailable to the decoder, and to adapt the output of a general-purpose MT system to the lexicon/style requested in a specific application domain.

The APE task usually demands human-annotated triplets since it is trained with tuples of *src* (source sentence), *mt* (machine translated sentence) and *pe* (post-edited sentence). Due to the fact that the post-edited sentences require professional translators to manually annotate *src-mt* pairs, the APE task is somewhat regarded as a data-scarce task. With only thousands of training examples provided, it's challenging to train a generation model and achieve satisfactory performance.

Previous works [15,23,33] have already demonstrated significant progress with Transformer [31] based models on APE. Various methods have been also explored to deal with the problem of data scarcity. Some researchers propose

Y. Feng and C. Feng (Eds.): CCMT 2023, CCIS 1922, pp. 57–68, 2023.
https://doi.org/10.1007/978-981-99-7894-6_6

to create synthetic data by adopting different methods, such as transfer learning [9] and data augmentation [8,15,32]. However, the created data still suffers from the domain deviance and can only provide limited supervision. Other researchers choose different pretrained language models, such as BERT [5] and XLM-RoBERTa [3], as their backbone models in APE tasks [14,18,32]. However, these models are mostly encoder-only, and require architecture adaptation when applied to APE, degrading their performance.

This paper presents the system developed by HIT-MI&T Lab for the CCMT 2023 APE task of Chinese-English direction. In our work, we investigate several strategies to deal with data scarcity of APE. First, we choose mBART [17] as the backbone model and use the pretrained parameters to initialize both the encoder and the decoder. As mBART models learn massive multilingual knowledge during pre-training, they are reasonablely expected to adapted to APE by fine-tuning on only thousands of annotation data. Second, we create competitive synthetic triplets from openly-available parallel data using various techniques, including domain selection, forward translation [22] and data augmentation via large language model. We apply domain selection to the parallel data to bridge the domain gap with the real APE training data, then we try different MT models and do forward translation to generate synthetic mt on these chosen parallel data (which are deemed as synthetic src and pe). Considering that large language models (LLM) such as ChatGPT[1] has demonstrated strong capabilities in multiple NLP tasks, we also try the data augmentation with the help of LLM. At last, different models trained with different data are ensembled to achieve further improvement.

Experiments on the development set shows we obtain competitive results in this year's APE task, verifying the effectiveness of our proposed method.

Our contributions are summarized as follows:

- A mBART-based model with complete encoder-decoder pre-trained architecture is proposed for APE.
- The impact of domain and translation models is explored when generating synthetic data.
- As one of the most popular large language models, ChatGPT is tried to help our data augmentation.

2 Architecture

mBART is a sequence-to-sequence denoising auto-encoder pre-trained on large-scale monolingual corpora in many languages using the BART objective [16], and it presents the first method for pre-training a sequence-to-sequence model by denoising full texts in multiple languages [17]. Specifically, the input texts are noised by masking phrases and permuting sentences, and a single Transformer model is learned to recover the texts.

---

[1] https://openai.com/chatgpt.

Different from the encoder-only pre-trained models such as BERT, mBART is a model with complete encoder-decoder architecture and doesn't require architecture adaptation when applied to APE. In addition, mBART is pre-trained in many languages, thus holding a powerful cross-language representation ability. What's more, the denoising operation in the pre-training stage of mBART is very similar to the APE task, making mBART easy to correct the MT outputs to post-edits. Considering the above three points, we believe that mBART is naturally suitable for APE task. Therefore, we use mBART as the backbone model and use the pretrained parameters to initialize both the encoder and the decoder.

To use mBART for the APE task, as shown in Fig. 1, we concatenate the *src* and the *mt* with a special token *<SEP>* to form the input.

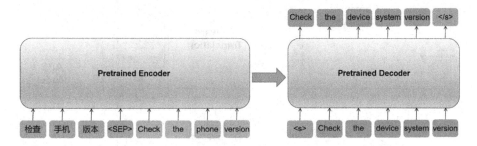

Fig. 1. Our proposed mBART-based APE model. The *src* and the *mt* are concatenated by the *<SEP>* symbol and fed to the encoder, the output of the decoder is expected to be the *pe*.

Given that combining the predictions from several models has proven to be an elegant approach for increasing the performance of the models [6], we use different models for ensemble and achieve further improvement in our final system.

3 Data Augmentation

3.1 Synthetic Data Generation

We believe that APE task is data-hungry as a generative task, so it's quite important to use the available parallel data to create synthetic data. In our synthetic data generation procedure, we apply domain selection to the parallel data and try different MT models to do forward translation.

Domain Selection. As our task is to perform APE on a specialized domain, incorporating data from various sources may be harmful to the performance. Therefore, we perform domain selection on the parallel data, and only include a domain-related portion to generate synthetic data.

To perform domain classification, we use the training triplets as in-domain data, and randomly sample general domain data from openly-available parallel data. We follow Huang et al. [7] to fine-tune BERT as a binary classifier and use it to score all parallel data on a continuous scale from zero to one, where score of zero means "domain-unrelated" and score of one means "domain-related". Then we select the most domain-related portion in the parallel data from high to low according to these scores. After that, we train a Transformer-based NMT to do forward translation and create the synthetic triplets. Finally, the synthetic triplets are combined with real triplets (which is oversampled) for training. The procedure is shown in Fig. 2.

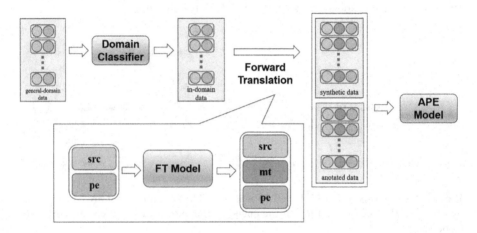

Fig. 2. The procedure of generating synthetic data. FT is abbreviation for Forward Translation.

Different MT Models. Due to differences in training data and architecture, the outputs of different MT models have various data distributions. Considering that the performance of MT models may affect the quality of the outputs, we try different MT models to generate synthetic data.

3.2   ChatGPT-Based Data Augmentation

ChatGPT is a large language model developed by OpenAI. It can achieve amazing performance and even surpass the state-of-the-art in many natural language processing tasks in zero shot settings, causing a huge sensation all over the world [26]. Therefore, we decide to try data augmentation with its help in the APE task.

AMT. Inspired by Yang et al. [33] and Oh et al. [23], we first use ChatGPT to generate *amt* (additional machine translations). Specifically, we obtain the *amt* with the help of ChatGPT, designing the prompt as follows:

```
Translate"{src}" into English:
```

Then, as shown in Fig. 3, we concatenate the *src*, the *mt* and the *amt* with a special token $<SEP>$ to form the input.

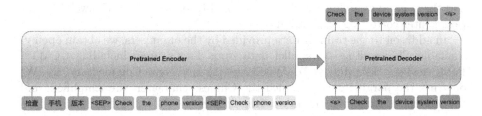

Fig. 3. The input and output of mBART model when we use ChatGPT to generate *amt*.

Direct APE. Besides, we also try to apply ChatGPT to perform APE task directly, and explore the impact of prompt and demonstration through experiments.

To start with, we design two prompts to explore their impact on the performance. One prompt asks ChatGPT to do a translation task:

```
Translate "{src}" into English:
```

The other prompt applies ChatGPT to APE task directly:

```
The following is an English translation for "{src}": "{mt}",
provide a better English translation for "{src}":
```

Previous research shows that a few annotated samples can improve the performance of LLM via In-context Learning [19, 21]. Therefore, we extend the prompt with a few annotated samples as demonstration. Triplets are selected from the training set, and filled in the same prompt, and then concatenated as prefix to be fed together.

4 Experiments

4.1 Set-Up

Dataset. CCMT 2023's APE task focuses on Chinese-English (Zh-En) language pair in the domain of information and communications technology (ICT). Participants are provided with a training set with 5000 instances, a development set with 1000 instances and a test set with 10000 instances. Each dataset consists of triplets of *src*, *mt* and *pe*. The source sentences come from Huawei Consumer Official Website[2], the MT outputs are generated with a black-box MT system and the post-edits are created by professional translators from Huawei Translation Center correcting MT outputs.

In addition to the training data provided by the organisers, we obtain openly-available Chinese-English parallel data from data sources including CCMT[3], ParaCrawl [1], WikiMatrix [27], WikiTitles [13] and News Commentary [13]. We only use the parallel data of which the Chinese characters are simplified, and the amount of these parallel data is about 25M.

Pre-processing. We use following steps to pre-process the 25M Chinese-English parallel data:

- Filter out duplicant sentences and empty sentences.
- Unify the encoding formats to UTF-8, convert fullwidth forms to halfwidth forms, and delete non-printable characters.
- Apply truecasing to the English sentences.
- Filter out sentence pairs of which the English-to-Chinese token ratio higher than 2.5 or lower than 0.4.

After the pre-processing procedure, we obtain about 20M filtered parallel data and use these data together with the real APE data in the training stage.

Evaluation Metrics. TER scores [28] and BLEU scores [25] are used as primary and secondary evaluation metrics respectively.

Training Details. Our Transformer-based model and mBART-based model are both implemented with fairseq [24]. The Transformer model we used is Transformer-big with 6 encoders and 6 decoders, and the hidden size is 8192 for FFN layers and 1024 for all other layers. We use the Adam [11] optimizer with a constant learning rate of 5e−4 for optimization. Parameters are being tuned with 4000 steps of learning rates warm-up, and the batch size is 8192 tokens. Besides, FP16 is used to accelerate training. The mBART model we used is mBART.cc25[4] with 12 encoder and decoder layers trained on 25 languages' monolingual corpus. We also use the Adam optimizer for optimization,

---

[2] https://consumer.huawei.com/.

[3] http://mteval.cipsc.org.cn:81/CCMT2023/index.html.

[4] https://dl.fbaipublicfiles.com/fairseq/models/mbart/mbart.cc25.v2.tar.gz.

but change the constant learning rate to 3e−5. Parameters are being tuned with 2500 steps of learning rates warm-up, and the batch size is 1024 tokens.

4.2 Results of Different Architectures

We first compare the mBART architecture with the Transformer-big architecture. The input format of Transformer-based model is identical to that of mBART-based model, but Transformer-based model is not pre-trained. As we can see in Table 1, with 5K real training triplets combined with 200K synthetic triplets, the mBART architecture outperforms the Transformer-big architecture by a large margin, showing the significance of pretrained parameters in APE task and the effectiveness of pre-training in alleviating data scarcity.

Table 1. Results on the development set of CCMT 2023 Chinese-English APE with different architectures. The baseline APE system is a "do-nothing" system that leaves all original *mt* unmodified as the final APE outputs.

Architecture	TER	BLEU
mBART	**51.09**	**44.95**
do-nothing	55.39	39.08
Transformer-big	64.90	34.02

4.3 Results of Data Augmentation

To perform domain classification, we use 5K training triplets as in-domain data, and randomly sample 50K general domain data from openly-available parallel data. Then, we adopt different data sizes in our experiments when selecting the domain-related data, and find that data size matters a lot. As shown in Table 2, we achieve the best result when incorporating 200K data. More data will lead to domain irrelevance while using less data is not enough for the improvement of the performance.

Moreover, we try to formulate the training as two stages, which are domain-irrelevant pre-training and domain-specific fine-tuning. Specifically, as shown in Table 2, we train mBART with 2M synthetic data for 5 epochs and then continue to train the model with 200K synthetic data for 15 epochs. Unexpectedly, it turns out that the model trained in this way performs worse than the model trained only with 200K synthetic data. The reason why this result occurs may be the catastrophic forgetting [12,20], which means mBART model learns too much domain-irrelevant information which leads to severe overfitting and parameter collapse, resulting in reduced performance even after training with more domain-specific data.

Table 2. Results on the development set of CCMT 2023 Chinese-English APE with different sizes of synthetic data. For different synthetic data sizes, the real data is oversampled different times. Notice that the experiment with 20M synthetic data only runs 5 epochs, due to its long running time and relatively low performance.

Architecture	Synthetic	Real	Epoch	TER	BLEU
mBART	20K	5K*4	20	51.24	44.43
mBART	200K	5K*10	20	**51.09**	**44.95**
mBART	2M	5K*20	20	51.99	44.40
mBART	20M	5K*20	5	51.95	43.97
mBART	2M	5K*20	5	51.35	44.66
	+200K	+5K*10	+15	51.50	44.68
do-nothing	–	–	–	55.39	39.08

Then, we explore three different MT models, namely OPUS-MT-ZH-EN [30], NLLB [4] and our own NMT model. The OPUS-MT-ZH-EN is based on Marian-NMT [10] and trained with parallel corpora collected in OPUS [29]. The NLLB is based on Transformer and trained with Flores-200 [4], NLLB-Seed [4] and NLLB-MD [4]. Our own NMT model is based on Transformer and trained with openly-available parallel data that we obtained. As shown in Table 3, we achieve the best result when using our own Transformer-based NMT to generate synthetic data. Because OPUS-MT-ZH-EN and NLLB are trained with general domain data, which deviate from the distribution of the to-be-edited data, they perform a little bit worse than our Transformer-based NMT model, which is trained with in-domain data.

Table 3. Results on the development set of CCMT 2023 Chinese-English APE with different synthetic data generated by different MT models.

Architecture	MT Model	TER	BLEU
mBART	Transformer	**51.09**	**44.95**
mBART	OPUS-MT-ZH-EN	51.27	44.66
mBART	NLLB	51.39	44.77
do-nothing	-	55.39	39.08

To explore the effect of ChatGPT-based data augmentation, we train models with 5K real training triplets combined with 200K synthetic triplets, and find out that the mBART architecture with *amt* is hard to outperform the one without *amt*. The results are shown in Table 4. We think it is because the quality of *amt* generated by ChatGPT is worse than the original *mt*, thus introducing some noise into the APE task and leading to the performance degradation.

Table 4. Results on the development set of CCMT 2023 Chinese-English APE with different input forms.

Architecture	AMT	TER	BLEU
mBART	no	**51.09**	**44.95**
mBART	yes	51.29	44.91

To investigate the reason why ChatGPT-based data augmentation will lead to performance degradation, we try to apply ChatGPT to perform APE task directly, and explore the impact of prompt and demonstration through experiments. The experiment result, as we can see in Table 5, demonstrates that no prompt brings satisfactory performance. What's more, although the demonstration can help improve the performance, unfortunately, it's still much worse than our mBART model.

Table 5. Results on the development set of CCMT 2023 Chinese-English APE with different demonstrations and prompts of ChatGPT-based APE methods.

Architecture	Prompt	Demonstration	TER	BLEU
ChatGPT	The following is an English translation for "{src}": "{mt}", provide a better English translation for "{src}":	yes	73.65	23.06
ChatGPT	The following is an English translation for "{src}": "{mt}", provide a better English translation for "{src}":	no	75.42	22.02
ChatGPT	Translate "{src}" into English:	no	73.67	20.86
mBART	–	–	**51.09**	**44.95**

To draw a conclusion, applying ChatGPT to APE directly seems to be ineffective. We believe the reason is that the dataset of the APE task have very strong domain specificity, but ChatGPT is more suitable for the tasks in general domain and lacks zero-shot ability in domain-specific tasks. As a result, even though ChatGPT is very powerful, it is still difficult for it to surpass our specially trained mBART model in this specific task.

4.4   Results of Multi-model Ensemble

At last, we use different models for ensemble and achieve further improvement. The results are shown in Table 6, showing that although some models will underperform solely, when combining multiple models, the errors of a single model will likely be compensated by other models. As a result, the final performance of the ensemble would be better than that of a single model.

Table 6. Results on the development set of CCMT 2023 Chinese-English APE with multi-model ensemble. Ensemble A use four models which are trained with 20K/200K/ 2M/20M synthetic data generated by our own NMT for 20/20/5/5 epochs for ensemble. Ensemble B use three models which are trained with 200K synthetic data generated by OPUS-MT-ZH-EN/NLLB/our own NMT for ensemble. Ensemble C use the top three single models which are trained with 200K/20K/200K synthetic data generated by OPUS-MT-ZH-EN/our own NMT/our own NMT for ensemble. Single model is the best model trained with 200K synthetic data generated by our own NMT.

Architecture	TER	BLEU
mBART (ensemble A)	**49.29**	**46.65**
mBART (ensemble B)	50.00	46.06
mBART (ensemble C)	50.00	46.00
mBART (single)	51.09	44.95

5   Conclusion

In this paper, we describe our submission to CCMT 2023 automatic post-editing task. We use mBART as the backbone model, and generate synthetic data by domain selection, forward translation and data augmentation via large language model to alleviate the problem of data-scarcity. To further improve the performance of our system, we adopt multi-model ensemble to obtain the final model. Experiment results on the development set demonstrate the effectiveness of our method.

In the future, we will extend our system from Chinese-English to other language pairs to verify the effectiveness of our proposed method. Besides, we will fine-tune large language model on domain-specific data to help improve the automatic post-editing in specific domain.

Acknowledgement. This work is supported by National Key RD Program of China (2020AAA0108000, 2020AAA0108005), National Natural Science Foundation of China (62276077, U1908216), Key RD Program of Yunnan (202203AA080004) and Shenzhen College Stability Support Plan (No. GXWD20220811170358002).

References

1. Bañón, M., et al.: Paracrawl: web-scale acquisition of parallel corpora. In: Proceedings of the 58th Annual Meeting of the Association for Computational Linguistics, pp. 4555–4567 (2020)
2. Chatterjee, R., Federmann, C., Negri, M., Turchi, M.: Findings of the WMT 2019 shared task on automatic post-editing. In: Proceedings of the Fourth Conference on Machine Translation (Volume 3: Shared Task Papers, Day 2), pp. 11–28 (2019)
3. Conneau, A., et al.: Unsupervised cross-lingual representation learning at scale. arXiv preprint arXiv:1911.02116 (2019)
4. Costa-jussà, M.R., et al.: No language left behind: scaling human-centered machine translation. arXiv preprint arXiv:2207.04672 (2022)

5. Devlin, J., Chang, M.W., Lee, K., Toutanova, K.: BERT: pre-training of deep bidirectional transformers for language understanding. arXiv preprint arXiv:1810.04805 (2018)

6. Ganaie, M.A., Hu, M., Malik, A., Tanveer, M., Suganthan, P.: Ensemble deep learning: a review. Eng. Appl. Artif. Intell. **115**, 105151 (2022)

7. Huang, H., et al.: BJTU-Toshiba's submission to CCMT 2021 QE and APE task. In: Su, J., Sennrich, R. (eds.) CCMT 2021. CCIS, vol. 1464, pp. 25–38. Springer, Singapore (2021). https://doi.org/10.1007/978-981-16-7512-6_3

8. Huang, X., Lou, X., Zhang, F., Mei, T.: Lul's WMT22 automatic post-editing shared task submission. In: Proceedings of the Seventh Conference on Machine Translation (WMT), pp. 689–693 (2022)

9. Huang, X., Xu, J., Sun, M., Liu, Y.: Transfer learning for sequence generation: from single-source to multi-source. In: Proceedings of the 59th Annual Meeting of the Association for Computational Linguistics and the 11th International Joint Conference on Natural Language Processing (Volume 1: Long Papers), pp. 5738–5750 (2021)

10. Junczys-Dowmunt, M., et al.: Marian: fast neural machine translation in C++. In: Proceedings of ACL 2018, System Demonstrations, pp. 116–121 (2018)

11. Kingma, D.P., Ba, J.: Adam: a method for stochastic optimization. arXiv preprint arXiv:1412.6980 (2014)

12. Kirkpatrick, J., et al.: Overcoming catastrophic forgetting in neural networks. Proc. Natl. Acad. Sci. **114**(13), 3521–3526 (2017)

13. Kocmi, T., et al.: Findings of the 2022 conference on machine translation (WMT22). In: Proceedings of the Seventh Conference on Machine Translation (WMT), pp. 1–45 (2022)

14. Lee, D.: Cross-lingual transformers for neural automatic post-editing. In: Proceedings of the Fifth Conference on Machine Translation, pp. 772–776 (2020)

15. Lee, J., Lee, W., Shin, J., Jung, B., Kim, Y.G., Lee, J.H.: Postech-etri's submission to the wmt2020 ape shared task: automatic post-editing with cross-lingual language model. In: Proceedings of the Fifth Conference on Machine Translation, pp. 777–782 (2020)

16. Lewis, M., et al.: BART: denoising sequence-to-sequence pre-training for natural language generation, translation, and comprehension. arXiv preprint arXiv:1910.13461 (2019)

17. Liu, Y., et al.: Multilingual denoising pre-training for neural machine translation. Trans. Assoc. Comput. Linguist. **8**, 726–742 (2020)

18. Lopes, A.V., Farajian, M.A., Correia, G.M., Trénous, J., Martins, A.F.: Unbabel's submission to the wmt2019 ape shared task: BERT-based encoder-decoder for automatic post-editing. arXiv preprint arXiv:1905.13068 (2019)

19. Lu, Q., Qiu, B., Ding, L., Xie, L., Tao, D.: Error analysis prompting enables human-like translation evaluation in large language models: a case study on chatGPT. arXiv preprint arXiv:2303.13809 (2023)

20. McCloskey, M., Cohen, N.J.: Catastrophic interference in connectionist networks: the sequential learning problem. In: Psychology of Learning and Motivation, vol. 24, pp. 109–165. Elsevier (1989)

21. Min, S., et al.: Rethinking the role of demonstrations: what makes in-context learning work? In: Proceedings of the 2022 Conference on Empirical Methods in Natural Language Processing, pp. 11048–11064. Association for Computational Linguistics, Abu Dhabi, United Arab Emirates, December 2022. https://aclanthology.org/2022.emnlp-main.759

22. Negri, M., Turchi, M., Chatterjee, R., Bertoldi, N.: Escape: a large-scale synthetic corpus for automatic post-editing. In: Proceedings of LREC 2018, Eleventh International Conference on Language Resources and Evaluation, pp. 24–30. European Language Resources Association (ELRA) (2018)
23. Oh, S., Jang, S., Xu, H., An, S., Oh, I.: Netmarble AI center's WMT21 automatic post-editing shared task submission. arXiv preprint arXiv:2109.06515 (2021)
24. Ott, M., et al.: fairseq: A fast, extensible toolkit for sequence modeling. In: Proceedings of the 2019 Conference of the North. Association for Computational Linguistics (2019)
25. Papineni, K., Roukos, S., Ward, T., Zhu, W.J.: BleU: a method for automatic evaluation of machine translation. In: Proceedings of the 40th Annual Meeting of the Association for Computational Linguistics, pp. 311–318 (2002)
26. Qin, C., Zhang, A., Zhang, Z., Chen, J., Yasunaga, M., Yang, D.: Is chatGPT a general-purpose natural language processing task solver? arXiv preprint arXiv:2302.06476 (2023)
27. Schwenk, H., Chaudhary, V., Sun, S., Gong, H., Guzmán, F.: Wikimatrix: mining 135m parallel sentences in 1620 language pairs from Wikipedia. In: Proceedings of the 16th Conference of the European Chapter of the Association for Computational Linguistics: Main Volume, pp. 1351–1361 (2021)
28. Snover, M., Dorr, B., Schwartz, R., Micciulla, L., Makhoul, J.: A study of translation edit rate with targeted human annotation. In: Proceedings of the 7th Conference of the Association for Machine Translation in the Americas: Technical Papers, pp. 223–231 (2006)
29. Tiedemann, J.: Parallel data, tools and interfaces in opus. In: Eight International Conference on Language Resources and Evaluation, 21–27 May 2012, Istanbul, Turkey, pp. 2214–2218 (2012)
30. Tiedemann, J., Thottingal, S.: Opus-mt-building open translation services for the world. In: Proceedings of the 22nd Annual Conference of the European Association for Machine Translation. European Association for Machine Translation (2020)
31. Vaswani, A., et al.: Attention is all you need. In: Advances in Neural Information Processing Systems, vol. 30 (2017)
32. Wang, J., et al.: Alibaba's submission for the WMT 2020 ape shared task: improving automatic post-editing with pre-trained conditional cross-lingual BERT. In: Proceedings of the Fifth Conference on Machine Translation, pp. 789–796 (2020)
33. Yang, H., et al.: HW-TSC's participation at WMT 2020 automatic post editing shared task. In: Proceedings of the Fifth Conference on Machine Translation, pp. 797–802 (2020)

A k-Nearest Neighbor Approach for Domain-Specific Translation Quality Estimation

Na Ye[✉] and Jiaxin Li

School of Computer Science, Shenyang Aerospace University, Shenyang 110136, China
yena_1@126.com

Abstract. Translation quality estimation (QE) is used to assess the quality of machine translation (MT) output without using reference translations. Although QE technology in general domain has made significant progress, it still faces challenges in specific domains due to limited data availability and expensive annotation costs. To address this issue, this paper proposes a kNN-QE method, which provides instance-based augmentation for the model by querying the built datastore during prediction. This method does not require an explicit training process and improves the prediction accuracy of the model without spending additional time and computing resources to train the model. This paper further improves the model performance by adjusting the loss function to alleviate the problem of QE data label bias. Experiments on two domain-specific datasets show that the proposed method achieves significant improvements over the baseline method on word-level QE tasks.

Keywords: Translation quality estimation · Domain-specific · kNN

1 Introduction

Machine translation quality estimation is the task of automatically assigning a quality score to machine translation output without relying on reference translations. The practical significance of QE lies in its ability to automatically identify and filter low-quality translations, thereby reducing operating costs and the workload of manual post-editing. According to the level of granularity of prediction, QE is generally categorized into sentence-level task and word-level task. Sentence-level QE aims to predict a single quality score by taking the entire source sentence and its translation as input. On the other hand, word-level QE is a more detailed task that aims to predict a binary quality label for all machine-translated words, expressing whether there are translation errors for each word and word intervals. This paper focuses on word-level QE.

In recent years, researchers have devoted themselves to promoting the development of QE technology. Kim et al. [1] propose a predictor-estimator framework, where the predictor is trained on a massively parallel corpus via an RNN-based encoder-decoder model to extract a quality vector for each word in the translation, which is then passed as input to the estimator. The estimator uses the sequential quality vector to predict the

Y. Feng and C. Feng (Eds.): CCMT 2023, CCIS 1922, pp. 69–80, 2023.
https://doi.org/10.1007/978-981-99-7894-6_7

translation quality through RNN to improve the accuracy and reliability of the results. Many subsequent studies have built upon this model, using it as a foundational framework. Patel et al. [2] suggested extracting quality characteristics by utilizing bilingual context windows in the RNN model. Li et al. [3] proposed to combine the two sub-networks of the predictor and the estimator into a complete neural network, called the unified neural network model. The "Bilingual Expert" model [4] proposed by Fan et al. is a further improvement of the prediction-estimation model. This model modifies the estimator from the original feedforward neural network to Bi-LSTM [5], which is closer to the actual application scenario. With the emergence of cross-language pre-training models, the information exchange between multiple languages has been promoted, so that a single model can be applied to tasks in multiple languages. The TransQuest [6] framework proposed by Ranasinghe et al. is based on the cross-language model XLM-R [7].

However, previous studies mostly focus on the estimation of translation quality in general domain and research on specific domains is still lacking. Domain-specific QE data are characterized by strong specialization and high complexity, which pose challenges to data acquisition and labeling. The scarcity of manually annotated QE data in specific domains results in insufficient training and hinders the models' ability to effectively learn data features and patterns.

To solve the problem of insufficient QE training data, some researchers use data enhancement methods to improve the effect of QE models. Kim et al. [1] and Liu et al. [8] use additional parallel data to train an additional machine translation system, and then take the output of the translation system and the reference as the training data for the QE model. Another method commonly used in data enhancement is to construct pseudo-data labels. Wu et al. [9] proposed to fit QE data error type distribution to automatically construct pseudo-data labels by adding errors to the machine translation results. The above methods rely on a certain amount and quality of parallel corpora. However, for specific fields, high-quality parallel data is also a very scarce resource. In addition, Kepler et al. [10] used an automatic post-editing (APE) system to generate pseudo-post-edited text and used the TERCOM[1] tool to automatically generate word-level and sentence-level quality labels. The pseudo-PE assisted QE method proposed by Wang et al. [11] also uses the APE system to generate pseudo-references. But for a specific domain, due to the specialty and particularity of the domain, there are few fully validated and adapted APE systems available.

This paper aims to address the aforementioned issues by incorporating a kNN module into the QE model. Through utilizing a nearest neighbor-based similarity measure, this method enables the model to effectively leverage a limited set of training samples to augment the QE system's classification prediction capabilities. First, construct a datastore with the QE data. Then perform k-nearest search on the datastore to retrieve k potential target representations and labels to assist in making the final decision for the current token. In addition, we modified the model's loss function to alleviate label distribution bias. Experimental results on two domain datasets show that our method achieves higher Matthew's correlation coefficient (MCC) [12] score than baseline methods.

---

[1] http://www.cs.umd.edu/~snover/terco/.

2 Proposed Method

2.1 Overall Architecture

We propose a kNN-based domain-specific translation quality estimation method kNN-QE, as shown in Fig. 1. This method obtains knowledge through the use of previously established instances during the inference process.

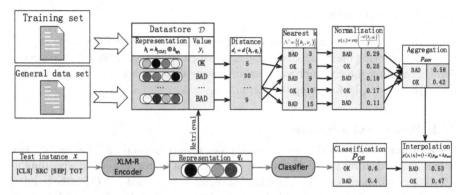

Fig. 1. An illustration of kNN-QE. The blue line denotes the workflow for original QE model and the black line denotes the workflow for kNN. (Color figure online)

In the above figure, the input sequence is the concatenation of the source language sentence and the target language sentence. This sequence is then encoded using the XLM-R encoder and generates hidden vector representations for each token in the input sequence. Afterward, the classifier is used to calculate the probabilities of the target sentence's tokens belonging to every class. Simultaneously, the hidden vector representation of the target token is used for querying the datastore in the kNN module, which computes the predicted probabilities based on nearest neighbors. Finally, the two probability distributions are interpolated to obtain the predicted labels.

2.2 XLM-R Encoder

Based on the Transformer [13] architecture, XLM-R [7] encoder can realize language representation learning across multiple languages to meet the needs of downstream tasks under limited training data. The XLM-R encoder is trained under a multi-lingual masked language modeling (MLM) [14] task, which leverages word embedding and position encoding layers to enable the model to adapt to words in different languages more effectively.

We take [CLS] SRC [SEP] TGT as our input sequence x, and each word of the target sentence is separated by <GAP>, which represents the gap between adjacent target words. XLM-R encodes x into vector h, which is the latent feature representation output by the last hidden layer of the encoder.

2.3 Classifier

We take the hidden vectors obtained through the XLM-R encoder and use the classifier to map them to the probabilities of different labels. For the classifier, we utilized XLMRobertaForTokenClassification, which is a linear layer used for token-level label classification in a sequence. This enables us to make classification predictions and assign corresponding labels to the predicted tokens.

2.4 k-Nearest Neighbor

kNN-QE integrates the nearest neighbor retrieval mechanism into the prediction stage of the model, allowing the model to directly access the built datastore for better reasoning during prediction, thereby improving performance without further training. Specifically, kNN-QE includes the following two steps.

2.4.1 Datastore Construction

The datastore consists of a set of key-value pairs. Construct datastore $\mathcal{D}$, where the key in the datastore stores the concatenation of the hidden vector $h_{[CLS]}$ corresponding to [CLS] in each training sample and the hidden vector of each token of TGT in the training sample, and the value stores the label $y \in \mathcal{Y} = \{OK, BAD\}$ of the token as follows:

$$h_i = h_{[CLS]} \oplus h_{tgt_i} \tag{1}$$

$$\mathcal{D} = \{(h_i, y_i)\}_{i=1}^{I} \tag{2}$$

where I is the number of tokens in the TGT part of the training sample plus the number of <GAP>, h_{tgt_i} is the hidden vector of the i th token in the TGT, h_i is the spliced hidden vector corresponding to the i th token in the training sample in the datastore.

2.4.2 Prediction

During prediction, kNN-QE aims to interpolate the probabilities predicted by the original QE model and the probabilities predicted by the kNN module. When predicting the label corresponding to the t th word, obtain the hidden vector corresponding to [CLS] of the sentence and the word to be predicted from the last hidden layer of the XLM-R encoder, and splice the two to obtain the query vector q_t, which is used to query the datastore for k nearest neighbors according to the l_2 distances. Denote the retrieved neighbors as $\mathcal{N} = \{(h_j, v_j), j \in \{1, 2, \ldots, k\}\}$. Convert it to a kNN distribution, where v_j is the label corresponding to h_j. Formally, the kNN distribution is constructed in the following way:

$$p_{kNN}(y_t|x_t) \propto \sum_{(h_j, v_j) \in \mathcal{N}} \mathbb{I}_{y_t=v_j} \exp\left(\frac{-d(h_j, q_t)}{T}\right) \tag{3}$$

where T is the temperature and d is the Euclidean distance function.

Finally, the kNN distribution is used to interpolate the distribution of the QE model to obtain more accurate prediction results.

$$p(y_t|x_t) = (1 - \lambda)p_{QE}(y_t|x_t) + \lambda p_{kNN}(y_t|x_t) \tag{4}$$

The hyperparameters for this approach are the number k of nearest neighbors, the interpolation constant λ, the temperature T, and the choice of datastore.

2.5 Loss Function

2.5.1 Weighted Cross-Entropy

During training, aiming at the problem of label imbalance in the training data, where the number of samples with the OK label is significantly greater than the number of samples with the BAD label. Such imbalances may result in biased predictions, where the model favors the OK label and performs poorly in predicting the BAD label. As a solution to this problem, we propose to modify the mean squared error loss function in model to a weighted cross-entropy loss function. We achieve this modification by adjusting the category weights, taking into account the relative proportions of OK and BAD samples in the dataset. This approach is aimed at emphasizing the importance of learning and predicting BAD-labeled samples during the training process. The formula for the proposed weighted cross-entropy loss function is presented as follows:

$$L = -\frac{1}{N}\sum_{i=1}^{N}\sum_{j=1}^{M} w_j y_{ij} \log(p_{ij}) \tag{5}$$

where N is the number of training samples, M is the number of categories, y_{ij} is the true label of the i th sample, p_{ij} is the predicted probability of the j th category of the i th sample, and w_j is the weight of the j th category.

To set the weights for the weighted cross-entropy loss function, we adopted a manual adjustment approach to ensure better focus on the performance of the BAD labels during training. We set the weight for the OK labels, which constitute a larger proportion of the samples, to 1. For the BAD labels, which represent a smaller proportion of the samples, we experimented with four different weight adjustment schemes:

1) Proportion Weighting Method: Divide the proportion of OK labels by the proportion of BAD labels.
2) Square Root Weighting Method: Divide the proportion of OK labels by the proportion of BAD labels, and take the square root of the result.
3) Logarithmic Weighting Method: Divide the proportion of OK labels by the proportion of BAD labels, and take the logarithm of the result.
4) Difference Weighting Method: Calculate the difference between the proportions of OK labels and BAD labels.

For the four different weight configurations mentioned above, we will select the one that performs best on the validation set for use in subsequent experiments.

3 Experiments

3.1 Datasets

We use two datasets for training and evaluation.

The first one is the manually annotated English-Chinese patent QE corpus (Patent_1) [15]. The dataset comprised 620 annotated QE triples (SRC, TGT, LABEL). SRC is the source patent text. TGT is the machine-translated text obtained from the free online Google translation engine[2]. We manually post-edited TGT and used the TERCOM tool to automatically acquire LABEL. Due to the Light PE principle adopted during post-editing, the label distribution of the corpus is imbalanced with the OK and BAD labels approximately following a ratio of 9:1.

The second one is the automatically constructed pseudo English-Chinese patent QE corpus (Patent_2). The dataset comprised 800 pseudo QE triples. SRC is the source patent text. TGT is the machine-translated text obtained from Google translation engine. We use the manual translation (not the post-edited version of TGT) provided by the European Patent Office to automatically acquire LABEL with the TERCOM tool. In this corpus, the ratio of OK to BAD labels was approximately 7:3.

We randomly split the above two corpora into training, validation, and test sets under a 7:1:2 ratio, respectively. The data statistics are illustrated in Table 1.

Table 1. Statistics of the datasets in our experiments.

Dataset	Data	Sentences
Patent_1	train	434
	dev	62
	test	124
Patent_2	train	560
	dev	80
	test	160

3.2 Settings

We use the Matthew's correlation coefficient (MCC) on the target side as the primary evaluation metric, and F1-OK and F1-BAD on the target side as secondary metrics.

We retrieve $k = 5$ neighbors and conduct experiments on $\lambda \in [0.1, 0.9]$ and $T \in \{2, 5, 7, 10, 12, 15\}$ to select the hyperparameters λ and T for each method and dataset. Our kNN strategy adopts different data types and data volumes when constructing the datastore.

We use Adam to optimize our networks, the batch size is set to 8, and the learning rate is set to 2e-5. For all experiments, we employed the NVIDIA Tesla T4 GPU for computational purposes.

---

[2] https://translate.google.com/.

3.3 Results and Analysis

3.3.1 Results of k-Nearest Neighbor Module

Table 2 shows the experimental results on two datasets after adding the kNN module to the baseline model [5] (Base QE). Base QE is trained only using the domain-specific training data. As for the datastore, we use the same training set. For further comparison, we also tried to use the data in the general-domain (from WMT2020 QE word-level task) [16] as the datastore. We conducted experiments with 500, 750 and 1000 instances.

Table 2. The MCC scores of different models on two datasets.

Models	Datastore	Patent_1			Patent_2		
		MCC	F1-OK	F1-BAD	MCC	F1-OK	F1-BAD
Base QE		24.51	**96.91**	14.16	22.49	87,66	26.44
+kNN	domain-specific training set	23.81	96.89	14.10	25.72	**87.86**	30.48
	500 (general)	24.68	96.90	14.89	30.16	86.64	42.36
	750 (general)	25.50	96.72	23.03	32.94	86.22	46.61
	1000 (general)	**26.04**	96.87	**25.43**	**33.25**	87.04	**47.12**

We can see that after adding the kNN module, We can see that after adding the kNN module, the model's MCC score improved by 1.53% and 10.76% compared to the baseline model. It is worth noting that the magnitude of the improvement is obviously different on different datasets. This may be attributed to the significant bias of the training data labels in the Patent_1 dataset. Such bias results in inadequate model training. Since the kNN module does not directly participate in training, but uses trained parameters for prediction, it is still limited by the imperfection of the model caused by insufficient data in the training phase and cannot give full play to its performance. Furthermore, by examining the experimental results for F1-OK and F1-bad, we can discern that the incorporation of the KNN module significantly enhances the predictive performance for the BAD label. Even though there may be a slight sacrifice in predictive performance for the OK label, this improvement still contributes greatly to the overall effectiveness. The F1 score for the BAD label has improved by 11.27%.

In addition, from the experimental results we can observe that the datastore composed of general domain data is more helpful to improve the performance of the model. Through experimental results, we believe that building a datastore with general domain data can help balance the label bias problem. General domain datasets can provide more samples of BAD labels, thus helping to balance the label distribution. Additionally, the experimental effects reveal an improvement trend with an increase in data volume in the datastore. However, it is important to note that as the amount of data increases, the computational complexity of the model also increases. Therefore, it is necessary to carefully evaluate the impact of data volume and computational complexity, rather than blindly expanding the data volume in the datastore.

3.3.2 Results of Weighted Cross-Entropy Loss Function

Table 3 presents the experimental results on two datasets using the weighted cross-entropy loss function.

Table 3. The MCC scores of using weighted cross-entropy loss function on two datasets.

Models	Patent_1			Patent_2		
	MCC	F1-OK	F1-BAD	MCC	F1-OK	F1-BAD
Base QE	24.51	**96.91**	14.16	22.49	**87,66**	26.44
+weighted cross-entropy	**37.20**	95.29	**41.37**	**34.68**	80.46	**51.11**

The results indicate that modifying the loss function leads to a considerable enhancement in addressing the issue of label bias in the training data. Compared to the baseline model, we observed an increase in the MCC scores of 12.69% and 12.19% for their respective datasets. Additionally, the F1-BAD scores increased by 27.21% and 24.67% for two datasets. These results suggest that the adoption of the weighted cross-entropy loss function enables the model to better cope with label bias by assigning more weight to categories with larger biases, thereby allowing the model to focus more on these categories and improve its accuracy in classifying them.

3.3.3 Results of the Fused Method

Table 4 presents the experimental results derived from the integration of the aforementioned two approaches.

The kNN-QE model after adding the kNN module to the model with the modified loss function achieved significant improvements in MCC scores of 1.11% and 6.74%, and F1-BAD scores of 1.06% and 5.79%, respectively. It is worth noting that, unlike the experimental results in Table 2, we use data in the domain to build a datastore at this time, and this improves the model effect more significantly. Our analysis is that when the model is relatively stable, the data in the domain is closer to the actual application scenario, consistent with the data distribution in the target domain, and has higher data quality and reliability. In this way, the model can acquire a more accurate understanding of the characteristics and patterns of the target domain, thereby facilitating the prediction precision of the model in that domain.

3.4 Results After Integrating Domain Transfer Method

In this paper, we also investigate the effect of domain transfer on kNN-QE using broader QE data in general-domains. We first train the original QE model using the QE training data from the WMT20 word-level task [16]. Then, we fine-tune the model using QE data specific to the target domain, enabling us to obtain a domain-adapted QE model through domain transfer. Table 5 gives the comparative results.

Table 4. The MCC scores of applying the kNN module and weighted cross-entropy loss function on two datasets.

Models	Datastore	Patent_1			Patent_2		
		MCC	F1-OK	F1-BAD	MCC	F1-OK	F1-BAD
Base QE		24.51	**96.91**	14.16	22.49	**87.66**	26.44
+weighted cross-entropy		37.20	95.29	41.37	34.68	80.46	51.11
kNN-QE	domain-specific training set	**38.31**	95.66	**42.43**	**41.42**	82.87	**56.90**
	500 (general)	37.47	95.21	41.58	40.71	79.67	55.08
	750 (general)	37.77	95.37	41.90	40.82	79.71	55.14
	1000 (general)	37.91	95.43	42.01	41.01	80.31	56.24

Table 5. The MCC scores of kNN-QE after integrating domain transfer method on two datasets.

Models	Datastore	Patent_1			Patent_2		
		MCC	F1-OK	F1-BAD	MCC	F1-OK	F1-BAD
Base QE (domain transfer)		44.03	97.33	39.51	29.12	84.71	44.39
+kNN	domain-specific training set	46.41	97.38	43.12	34.42	84.44	49.76
	500 (general)	44.90	**97.40**	41.98	34.25	84.40	49.63
	750 (general)	43.99	97.32	39.86	34.15	84.39	49.25
	1000 (general)	43.30	97.27	39.11	34.17	84.34	49.59
+weighted cross-entropy		49.11	97.05	51.69	36.52	85.73	50.77
kNN-QE	domain-specific training set	**50.20**	96.73	**54.03**	**41.81**	**85.66**	**55.64**
	500 (general)	49.28	97.07	51.82	41.49	85.51	55.43
	750 (general)	49.55	97.01	51.99	41.45	85.50	55.39
	1000 (general)	49.72	97.06	52.37	41.54	85.51	55.46

Through the experimental results, we can find that after domain transfer, kNN-QE can also achieve a certain improvement. Consistent with the previous analysis, in a more robust model, incorporating the kNN module and constructing the datastore with in-domain data have shown to provide the greatest assistance to the model. It is worth noting that when only the kNN module is added to the experiment on the patent_1 data set, if the datastore chooses data in the general-domains, it may lead to a decrease in model performance. We believe that there are certain differences in the sample distributions between general-domain data and in-domain data. These differences in the feature space can prevent the model from accurately selecting nearest neighbor samples, thereby affecting its performance.

3.5 Effects of the KNN Parameters

In addition, we investigated the impact of parameters λ and T in the KNN-QE model under different data set constructions of the datastore. Figure 2(a) displays the MCC value curves when using the KNN module with $\lambda \in [0.1, 0.9]$ on the patent_2 dataset, with $T = 10$ and $k = 5$. Meanwhile, Fig. 2(b) presents the MCC value curves on the patent_2 dataset with $\lambda = 0.7$ and $k = 5$, while varying $T \in \{2, 5, 7, 10, 12, 15\}$ using the KNN module.

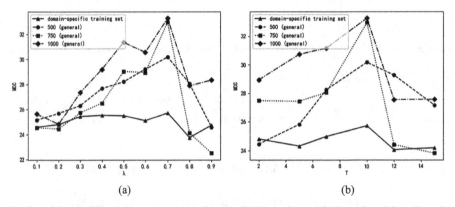

(a)   (b)

Fig. 2. (a)The MCC value curves when using the KNN module with $T = 10$ and $k = 5$ on the patent_2 dataset for $\lambda \in [0.1, 0.9]$. (b)The MCC value curves when using the KNN module with $\lambda = 0.7$ and $k = 5$ on the patent_2 dataset for $T \in \{2, 5, 7, 10, 12, 15\}$.

From Figs. 2(a) and 2(b), we can observe that MCC values show an upward trend with increasing λ and T, reaching their optimal values at $\lambda = 0.7$ and $T = 10$, respectively. This demonstrates that the KNN module contributes more compared to the baseline model. It is worth noting that the trends in MCC values are similar across different Datastore construction scenarios. This indicates that KNN-QE can maintain stable performance across different datasets.

4   Conclusion

In this paper, we propose kNN-QE, which aims to address the problem of insufficient training data in domain-specific translation quality estimation tasks. Different from the method of data enhancement, this paper uses kNN, an example-based learning method, to select the nearest k neighbors by calculating the distance between the sample to be predicted and the training sample to improve the accuracy of the prediction. At the same time, we also use the weighted cross-entropy loss function to alleviate the problem of label category imbalance. By assigning appropriate weights to samples from different classes, the model can be better trained to handle imbalanced datasets and improve its predictive power for minority classes.

Experiments demonstrate that our method can achieve remarkable predictive performance with limited training data. From the experimental results, it was observed that the effect of model training has a significant influence on the selection of appropriate data for creating a datastore. If the model can reach a stable and high-performance state in the early training stage, it will be more helpful to choose data in the domain that is similar to the target task and can provide more useful information to build the datastore. Conversely, it might be more suitable to select a general-domain dataset that contains a vast amount of data and has broader coverage. Furthermore, we investigate the effect of domain transfer on the model and demonstrate that the performance of kNN-QE has been further improved after using general-domain data for pre-training. We also explored the impact of parameters within the KNN module on the model's performance.

In future research, we will continue to explore methods for optimizing domain-specific translation quality estimation tasks. We will further study and improve the kNN-QE model to increase the performance and generalization ability of the model.

Acknowledgements. This work is supported by the National Natural Science Foundation of China (U1908216), the Humanity and Social Science Foundation for the Youth Scholars of Ministry of Education of China (19YJC740107), and the Project supported by the Science and Technology Plan of Shenyang City, China (20-202-1-28).

References

1. Kim, H., Jung, H.Y., Kwon, H., Lee, J.H., Na, S.H.: Predictor-estimator: neural quality estimation based on target word prediction for machine translation. ACM Trans. Asian Low-Resour. Lang. Inf. Process. **17**(1), 1–22 (2017). https://doi.org/10.1145/3109480
2. Patel, R.N., Sasikumar, M.: Translation quality estimation using recurrent neural network. In: Proceedings of the First Conference on Machine Translation: Volume 2, Shared Task Papers, pp. 819–824 (2016)
3. Li, M., Xiang, Q., Chen, Z., Wang, M.: A unified neural network for quality estimation of machine translation. IEICE Trans. Inf. Syst. **101**(9), 2417–2421 (2018)
4. Fan, K., Wang, J., Li, B., Zhou, F., Chen, B., Si, L.: Bilingual expert can find translation errors. In: Proceedings of the AAAI Conference on Artificial Intelligence, vol. 33, pp. 6367–6374 (2019)
5. Graves, A., Schmidhuber, J.: Framewise phoneme classification with bidirectional LSTM and other neural network architectures. Neural Netw. **18**(5–6), 602–610 (2005)
6. Ranasinghe, T., Orasan C., Mitkov R.: TransQuest: Translation quality estimation with cross-lingual transformers. In: arXiv preprint arXiv:2011.01536 (2020)
7. Conneau, A., Khandelwal, K., Goyal, N., et al.: Unsupervised cross-lingual representation learning at scale. In: Jurafsky, D., Chai, J., Schluter, N., Tetreault, J.R. (eds.) Proceedings of the 58th Annual Meeting of the Association for Computational Linguistics, ACL 2020, Online, pp. 8440–8451 (2020)

8. Liu, L., Fujita, A., Utiyama, M., Finch, A., Sumita, E.: Translation quality estimation using only bilingual corpora. IEEE/ACM Trans. Audio Speech Lang. Process. **25**(9), 1762–1772 (2017)

9. Wu, H., Yang, M., Wang, J., Zhu, J., Zhao, T.: Target oriented data generation for quality estimation of machine translation. In: Natural Language Processing and Chinese Computing: 8th CCF International Conference, NLPCC 2019, pp. 393–405 (2019)

10. Kepler, F., Trénous, J., Treviso, M., et al.: Unbabel's participation in the WMT19 translation quality estimation shared task. In: Processing of the 4th Conference on Machine Translation, pp. 78–84 (2019)

11. Wang, M., Yang, H., Shang, H., et al.: HW-TSC's participation at WMT 2020 quality estimation shared task. In: Proceedings of the Fifth Conference on Machine Translation, pp. 1056–1061 (2020)

12. Matthews B W.: Comparison of the predicted and observed secondary structure of T4 phage lysozyme. Biochimica et Biophysica Acta (BBA)-Protein Struct. **405**(2), 442–451 (1975)

13. Vaswani, A., Shazeer, N., Parmar, N., et al.: Attention is all you need. Adv. Neural Inf. Process. Syst. **30** (2017)

14. Devlin, J., Chang, M.W., Lee, K., Toutanova, K.: BERT: pre-training of deep bidirectional transformers for language understanding. In: Proceedings of the 2019 Conference of the North American Chapter of the Association for Computational Linguistics: Human Language Technologies, Volume 1 (Long and Short Papers), pp. 4171–4186 (2019)

15. Ye, N., Jiang, L., Ma, D., Zhang, Y., Zhao, S., Cai, D.: Predicting post-editing effort for English-Chinese neural machine translation. In: 2021 International Conference on Asian Language Processing (IALP), pp. 154–158. IEEE (2021)

16. Specia, L., Blain, F., Fomicheva, M., et al.: Findings of the WMT 2020 shared task on quality estimation. In: Proceedings of the Fifth Conference on Machine Translation, pp. 743–764 (2020)

WSA: A Unified Framework for Word and Sentence Autocompletion in Interactive Machine Translation

Na Ye$^{(\boxtimes)}$ and Gen Fu

School of Computer Science, Shenyang Aerospace University, Shenyang 110136, China
yena_1@126.com

Abstract. Interactive machine translation (IMT) is a process that leverages collaboration between human translators and machine translation models to produce high-quality translations and improve translation efficiency. Automatic completion is a critical function of IMT, which generates alternative translation for inappropriate words or segments based on human feedback for the translation. There are two limitations in previous research on autocompletion. Firstly, they treat these two types of autocompletion tasks as independent tasks, thus ignoring the potential correlation between them. The second limitation is that they only focus on completing translations based on human feedback, ignoring the role of the initial translation. In this paper, we propose a novel word and sentence autocompletion (WSA) method, which jointly models word and sentence autocompletion tasks. By means of joint modeling, the proposed method not only enables the generation of translations at both word and sentence level, but also increases the accuracy of the translations. In addition, we further improve the accuracy of translation autocompletion by utilizing the initial translation to enhance the semantic representation of the source sentence. Experimental results show that our method significantly outperforms the baselines by 10.34% in accuracy for word-level task and 1.86 BLEU score for sentence-level task.

Keywords: Interactive Machine Translation · Autocompletion · Joint Modeling

1 Introduction

With the tremendous advances in neural network architecture and computing power, neural machine translation (NMT) has achieved significant progress in recent years [1–3]. Nevertheless, NMT systems still cannot satisfy the requirements in real applications with strict translation quality (eg., translating legal documents, medical reports, operating manual, academic papers). The most common method of producing high-quality translations is post-editing, which requires translators to modify machine translations, but this method is quite inefficient. Therefore, it is necessary to combine the high quality of human translators and the high efficiency of machine translation, and interactive machine translation attracts the attention of researchers [4–8]. IMT is an iterative process of collaboration between human translators and machine translation models until generating satisfactory translation results.

Y. Feng and C. Feng (Eds.): CCMT 2023, CCIS 1922, pp. 81–93, 2023.
https://doi.org/10.1007/978-981-99-7894-6_8

Autocompletion plays a crucial role in interactive machine translation, which suggests translation results according to text pieces from human feedback. Autocompletion can be divided into word and sentence autocompletion. Word autocompletion aims to complete the target word based on the source sentence, the translation context provided by human translators and the human typed characters [4, 9–12]. And sentence autocompletion aims to regenerate a better segment translation based on the source sentence and the translation context provided by human translators [8, 10, 13]. In sentence autocompletion task, human typed characters are not needed, and the segment between the left and right context is considered to be incorrect and needs to be regenerated. Figure 1 shows an example for word and sentence autocompletion.

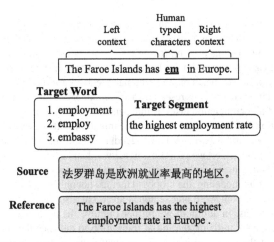

Fig. 1. An example for word and sentence autocompletion.

For autocompletion tasks, if the sentence autocompletion model produces correct translation, the target word of word autocompletion task must be in the target segment. However, previous research overlooked such potential correlation between the optimization goals of sentence and word autocompletion. Besides, although the initial translation may be different from the reference translation, it still can be a correct or partly correct translation which reflects the meaning of the source sentence. But previous research focused on generating translations based on human feedback, ignoring the role of the initial translation.

In this paper, we propose an effective and novel method called WSA which jointly models word and sentence autocompletion tasks. In addition, we enhance the representation of the source sentence by the initial translation to improve the performance of autocompletion. Experimental results show that the method achieves better results than strong baselines. The main contributions of this paper are as follows: (1) This is the first work to explore joint modeling of word and sentence autocompletion tasks. (2) We propose two joint modeling strategies, namely share-all-parameters (SAP) and share-encoder-parameters (SEP) to generate the target word and the target segment translation.

Both strategies improved the translation quality. (3) We explore the role of initial translation in interactive machine translation. The accuracy of the target translation is further improved by enhancing the source representation by the initial translation.

2 Related Work

Interactive machine translation has been widely employed to improve translation quality and efficiency. With the development of machine translation technology, many effective interactive machine translation methods have been proposed. Among these methods, word and sentence autocompletion are the most related work to our research.

Word Autocompletion. Langlais et al. [4] designed the first word autocompletion system by statistical ma-chine translation technology. Santy et al. [10] use constraint beam search to generate target word that match the characters typed by the user based on Transformer [2]. And Transformer only generate the next word of translation prefix, which limits their applications in practical scenarios. Huang et al. [11] propose a novel translation input method CoCat to generate target word based on source sentence and human typed characters. However, this method lacks the use of translation context, which limits the accuracy of target word prediction. To overcome these limitations, Li et al. [9] replaced the Transformer auto-regressive attention layer by a bidirectional attention module, so that the model can use the rightward information. In addition, the authors consider several types of translation context and use joint training strategy for all translation context types. Inspired by previous work on terminology control, Ailem et al. [12] consider human typed characters as a constraint and combine source sentence, human typed characters and translation context as the source side of training data.

Sentence Autocompletion. Prefix-constrained decoding is a traditional sentence autocompletion method, which completes suffix translation based on the prefix confirmed by human [10]. Lexically constrained decoding (LCD) also belongs to sentence autocompletion method. By extending beam search, LCD can leverage pre-specified translation to constrain NMT [13, 14], but this increases the decoding time. Therefore, Soft LCD has attracted the attention of many researchers. Weng et al. [15] propose a sequential bi-directional decoder to fix translation mistakes. The sequential bi-directional decoder consists of two decoders in opposite directions, so the model only uses partial constraints which reduces translation quality. Xiao et al. [8] turn sentence autocompletion to bilingual text filling task, which aims to fill missing segments in human feed-back translation. The method can be seemed as a sequence-to-sequence task whose decoding efficiency is higher than LCD.

However, the above research treats word and sentence autocompletion as independent tasks. In contrast, we improve translation quality by jointly modeling word and sentence autocompletion tasks and our model can not only generate target word but also target segment translation. In addition, the above methods only focus on using human feedback translation or lexically constrained information to generate translations, ignoring the role of initial translations. We incorporated the initial translation into interactive machine translation and achieved better translation results.

3 Proposed Method

3.1 Task Definition

Given the source sentence $x = \{x_1, x_2, ..., x_m\}$, the human typed characters $a = \{a_1, a_2, ..., a_k\}$ and the translation context $c = (c_l, c_r)$ where $c_l = \{c_{l,1}, c_{l,2}, ..., c_{l,i}\}$ and $c_r = \{c_{r,1}, c_{r,2}, ..., c_{r,j}\}$. The translation pieces c_l and c_r are on the left and right hand side of a, respectively. The word autocompletion task refers to predicting a target word w between c_l and c_r and the target word w may not be contiguous with the translation context c. The sentence autocompletion task refers to generating a target segment $s = \{s_1, s_2, ..., s_T\}$ between c_l and c_r, as depicted in Fig. 1. And the model parameters are θ. The conditional probability of word autocompletion is $p(w \mid x, c, a; \theta)$, and that of sentence autocompletion is as follows:

$$p(s|x, c; \theta) = \prod_{t=1}^{T} p(s_t|s_{<t}, x, c; \theta) \tag{1}$$

3.2 The Joint Model

We design two joint models for WSA as shown in Fig. 2. When the input does not contain human typed characters, the output of the models is the target segment, while when it contains human typed characters, the output of the models is the target word.

SAP Model. We transform word and sentence autocompletion into a unified conditional generation task. Therefore, we use the augmented dataset which combines both word-level and sentence-level datasets to train a Transformer model. The model consists of an encoder and a decoder. The encoder and decoder are composed to a stack of L identical layers and we set L to 6. The encoder encodes the embedding of the word-level and sentence-level inputs and outputs contextualized source representations. Compared to the encoder, the decoder has an additional cross-attention sublayer to attend the source representations, generating the next token based on the previously generated tokens. The hidden states of the SAP model are calculated as:

$$H^l = ShareEncLayer\left(H^{l-1}\right) \tag{2}$$

$$S^l = ShareDecLayer\left(S^{l-1}, H^L\right) \tag{3}$$

where H^l is the output of the l th shared encoder layer, S^l is the output of the l th shared decoder layer.

SEP Model. Similar to the SAP model, SEP model has the architecture of encoder-decoder. In contrast, SEP model has two independent decoders, one is the word-level decoder for generating the target word and the other one is the sentence-level decoder for generating the target segment translation. We use $<mask>$ token to identify whether the current input belongs to the word level or sentence level and use the corresponding decoder. The hidden states of the SEP model are calculated as:

$$H^l = ShareEncLayer\left(H^{l-1}\right) \tag{4}$$

$$S_w^l = WordDecLayer\left(S_w^{l-1}, H_w^L\right) \tag{5}$$

$$S_s^l = SegmentDecLayer\left(S_s^{l-1}, H_s^L\right) \tag{6}$$

where S_w^l is the output of the l th word decoder layer, S_s^l is the output of the l th sentence decoder layer, H_w^L and H_s^L are the contextualized source representations from H^L.

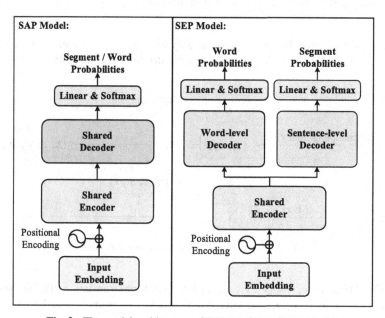

Fig. 2. The model architecture of SAP Model and SEP Model.

3.3 The Use of Initial Translation

We train an NMT model based on Transformer to obtain the initial translation i. Previous research has shown that using an additional encoder to extract representations of additional textual information is not as effective as input augmentation in which the source input is extended by the initial translation, so we adopt input augmentation to enhance the source representation. Figure 3 shows the input of WSA.

3.4 Training Data Construction

As we use the initial translation i to improve the effectiveness of autocompletion, the word-level training data $\mathcal{D}_w$ is a set of $\{(x, c, a, w, i)\}$ and the sentence-level training data $\mathcal{D}_s$ is a set of $\{(x, c, s, i)\}$.

During the training process, we require a large number of samples which ideally should be from professional translators. However, this approach can be cost-prohibitive.

Word-level input: 还有 给 棕熊 的 捐款 ⟨sep1⟩ And ⟨m⟩ ⟨mask⟩ ⟨c⟩ d o ⟨/c⟩ the
bears ⟨sep2⟩ and a contribution to the bear .
Target Word: donation
Sentence-level input: 还有 给 棕熊 的 捐款 ⟨sep1⟩ And ⟨mask⟩ the bears ⟨sep2⟩
and a contribution to the bear .
Target Translation: a donation for

Fig. 3. An example of the input of WSA. *<sep1>*, *<m>*, *<c>*, *</c>* and *<sep2>* are special
tokens used as delimiters. *<mask>* represents the unknown target word.

Therefore, we adopted the method proposed by Li et al. [9] to automatically construct
$\mathcal{D}_w$ and $\mathcal{D}_s$. Figure 4 shows the procedure of constructing training data.

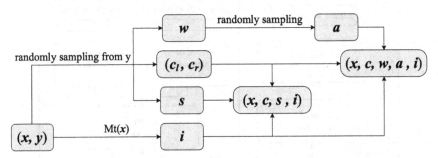

Fig. 4. The procedure of constructing train data

In the above figure, $y = \{y_1, y_2, ..., y_n\}$ is the reference translation of x. We randomly
sample a target word $w = y_p$ from y. We also randomly sample translation contexts
$c_l = y_{u1:u2}$, $c_r = y_{d1:d2}$ where $0 < u_1 < u_2 < p$ and $p < d_1 < d_2 < n$, the target segment
translation $s = y_{u2:d1}$. We also randomly preserve the first k characters of the target word
as human typed characters, where k is a random integer between one and half of the
length of the target word. Because the randomly sampled data contained many common
meaningless words (eg., the, that, in), we removed samples with target word less than
4 characters according to a certain proportion. In practical applications, the left context
c_l and the right context c_r can be empty. For every sample, we build all four types of
contexts: Zero-context: both c_l and c_r are empty; Prefix: The c_r is empty here; Suffix:
The c_l is empty here; Bi-context: sample c_l as in prefix, and sample c_r as in suffix.

3.5 Training

Given the word-level data $\mathcal{D}_w = \{(x, c, a, w, i)\}$ and the sentence-level data $\mathcal{D}_s =
\{(x, c, s, i)\}$, the goal of word-level and sentence-level training is to minimize the loss:

$$\mathcal{L}(\mathcal{D}_w; \theta) = -\sum_{(x,c,a,w,i)\in\mathcal{D}_w} log\, P(w|x, c, a, i; \theta) \tag{7}$$

$$\mathcal{L}(\mathcal{D}_s; \theta) = -\sum_{(x,c,s,i)\in\mathcal{D}_s} log\, P(s|x, c, i; \theta) \tag{8}$$

Since we jointly model the word and sentence autocompletion tasks, the train dataset $\mathcal{D} = \mathcal{D}_w + \mathcal{D}_s$ and our ultimate optimization goal is to minimize the following loss:

$$\mathcal{L}(\mathcal{D}; \theta) = \mathcal{L}(\mathcal{D}_w; \theta) + \mathcal{L}(\mathcal{D}_s; \theta) \tag{9}$$

4 Experiments

4.1 Datasets

We carry out experiments on both word and sentence autocompletion tasks in Chinese-English translation direction. The datasets are the same as Xiao et al. [8], consisting of approximately 2 million bilingual sentences collected from multiple online news websites. We constructed synthetic bilingual parallel sentence pairs based on the dataset using the method described in Sect. 3.4. Then we get equal-sized datasets for both word and sentence autocompletion tasks as shown in Table 1. We use Byte Pair Encoding to process the dataset.

Table 1. Data statistics for WSA on Chinese-English translation task. (Augmented: a combination of word-level and sentence-level dataset.)

Dataset	Bi-context	Prefix	Suffix	Zero-context	Sum	Augmented
Train	1.2M	1.2M	1.2M	1.2M	4.9M	9.8M
Dev	1254	1224	1279	1230	4987	9974
Test	1275	1263	1245	1237	5020	10040

4.2 Systems for Comparison

GWLAN (Li et al. 2021 [9]). We choose GLWAN as the first baseline. GLWAN is the first public benchmark in word autocompletion task. GLWAN not use Byte Pair Encoding to process the dataset. GLWAN has a Transformer encoder to encode the source sentence and also has a cross-lingual encoder. The cross-lingual encoder is similar to the Transformer decoder, while the only difference is that they replace the auto-regressive attention layer. The input of cross-lingual encoder is the concatenate of the translation piece c_l, the [MASK] token and the translation piece c_r. Finally, the model output the probability distribution of the [MASK] token. GLWAN set the probability of tokens not starting with human input characters to 0 and choose the token with the highest probability as the target word.

LCM (Ailem et al. 2022 [12]). Ailem propose to treat the human typed characters as a constraint to predict the right word starting by the latter. To do so, the source side of the training data consist of source sentence, the human typed characters, the [MASK] token and the translation context and they add different tags to delimiters each other. They use Transformer Encoder encode the source input and the decoder and use Transformer Decoder to generate the target word.

MT Model. We train an NMT model based on Transformer. The model is trained on the raw Zh-En dataset. As long as the predicted word appears in the machine translation result, we regard this case as correct.

BiTIIMT (Xiao et al. 2022 [8]). Inspired by BiTIIMT, we train a model to generate the missing segment in the translation based on Transformer, the source side of the training data is augmented with both the source sentence and the translation context.

WSA. Our WSA system include SAP model and SEP model. They were based on Transformer model and trained on both word-level dataset and sentence-level dataset mentioned in Sect. 3.3.

The WSA models and all baselines are based on the architecture with dmodel $= 512$, hidden $= 2048$, nheads $= 8$, nlayers $= 6$, and dropout $= 0.1$. We use Adam Optimizer with $\beta_2 = 0.9$, $\beta_2 = 0.98$, learning rate 5e–4 and stochastic gradient descent algorithm to train the models. We share all embedding parameters, use Gelus [16] as the activation function, adopt pre-layer normalization, set the maximum tokens in batch to 8192 and set gradient accumulation frequency to 4. We train all models on 2 NVIDIA Tesla T4 Tensor Core GPUs. Training stops until the maximum epochs is 80 or there was no performance improvement for 10 epochs. In the inference phase, the checkpoint used for testing is selected according to its performance on the valid dataset and we use the model to generate translation for testing data with a beam size of 10.

4.3 Evaluation Metrics

Following prior work [8, 9], we use three criteria to evaluate INMT systems. In the word autocompletion task, we choose accuracy as the evaluation metric. In the sentence autocompletion task, we employ BLEU [17] to measure translation quality and TER to measure efficiency, which is calculated by counting insertions, deletions, single word replacements and movements of consecutive word sequences.

$$Acc = N_{match}/N_{all} \qquad (10)$$

where N_{match} is the number of words that are correctly predicted and N_{all} is the number of testing examples, the edits include

4.4 Main Results

Table 2 and Table 3 present the comparative results of our methods and the baselines. WSA yields better results in both word and sentence autocompletion tasks compared with other baseline systems. The following tables use IT represent initial translation.

The results in Rows 1, 2 and 3 of Table 2 demonstrate that the MT Model outperforms GWLAN and LCM by at least $+ 3.7$ accuracy points on average. This can be attributed to the fact that we relaxed the requirements for the MT Model by considering a case as correct as long as the predicted word appears in the final MT result.

Table 2. The accuracy for the word autocompletion task.

Systems	Bi-context	Prefix	Suffix	Zero-context	Average
MT Model	65.67	65.67	65.67	65.67	65.67
GWLAN	55.42	55.21	52.28	47.53	52.61
LCM	63.18	63.13	63.05	58.52	61.97
WSA$_{(SAP + IT)}$	**73.28**	**75.13**	**71.88**	**68.95**	**72.31**

Table 3. The BLEU for the sentence autocompletion task.

Systems	Bi-context	Prefix	Suffix	Zero-context	Average
BiTIIMT	45.33	46.62	45.78	47.75	46.37
WSA$_{(SAP + IT)}$	**48.09**	**47.73**	**47.65**	**49.48**	**48.23**

Results in Row 2 and Row 3 of Table 2 show that the WSA method achieves an improvement up to 10.34 accuracy points compared to the LCM method on average. Even compared to the MT model with relaxed requirements, WSA still outperforms it by 6.64 accuracy points. Table 3 shows that compared to BiTIIMT, WSA achieves an improvement up to 1.86 BLEU. These findings verify our hypothesis that the word and sentence autocompletion tasks in interactive machine translation are correlated and the initial translation is beneficial for the final translation result.

5 Experimental Analysis

In this section, we present more detailed results on WSA and analyze the effects of joint modeling and initial translation. The following tables use IT represent initial translation. Table 4 and Table 5 give the results.

Table 4. The detailed results and accuracy for the word autocompletion task.

Systems	Bi-context	Prefix	Suffix	Zero-context	Average
LCM	63.18	63.13	63.05	58.52	61.97
WSA$_{(SAP)}$	**74.90**	74.58	71.56	66.20	71.81
WSA$_{(SEP)}$	73.58	74.11	**72.28**	63.37	70.83
LCM$_{(IT)}$	68.64	68.86	65.86	65.96	67.33
WSA$_{(SAP + IT)}$	73.28	**75.13**	71.88	**68.95**	**72.31**
WSA$_{(SEP + IT)}$	73.14	74.19	72.04	67.34	71.67

Table 5. The detailed results and BLEU for the sentence autocompletion task.

Systems	Bi-context	Prefix	Suffix	Zero-context	Average
BiTIIMT	45.33	46.62	45.78	47.75	46.37
WSA$_{(SAP)}$	46.09	46.69	46.41	48.17	46.84
WSA$_{(SEP)}$	46.68	46.94	46.62	48.22	47.12
BiTIIMT$_{(IT)}$	46.40	**47.88**	47.57	49.40	47.81
WSA$_{(SAP + IT)}$	**48.09**	47.73	**47.65**	**49.48**	**48.24**
WSA$_{(SEP + IT)}$	47.38	47.87	47.60	49.34	48.05

5.1 Effects of Joint Modeling

According to Table 4 and 5, SAP model and SEP model both outperform LCM by at least 8.86 accuracy points on word-level task, and outperform BiTIIMT by at least 0.47 BLEU on sentence-level task. This is because the shared encoder simultaneously encodes both the word-level and sentence-level inputs, obtaining more generalized encoding results and alleviating model overfitting, thus enhances the model's generalization ability.

Additionally, on word-level task, the SAP model generally outperforms the SEP model. This is because the sentence autocompletion task can assist the word autocompletion task. By sharing all parameters, our shared decoder has the ability to generate target segment translation, where the target word is highly likely to be included. Therefore, our model can fully understand the meaning represented by <mask>, then select the target word according to the human typed characters. However, the independent word-level decoder lacks the ability to fully understand the meaning of <mask>, and only knows that a word is missing at that position, then generates the target word based on the source text, context, and human typed characters. In zero-context situation, where there is a reduction in available information, it is more important to understand the meaning of <mask> and this increases the difference in performance between the two models.

Interestingly, the SEP model performs 0.28 BLEU better than the SAP model in the sentence autocompletion task. We think this is because target sentence autocompletion task does not require assistance from word-level autocompletion task. The model can inherently understand the contextual meaning and generate the correct target segment.

5.2 Effects of Initial Translation

Table 4 and 5 show that WSA performs better than the baselines by incorporating additional information from the initial translation, achieving an improvement of 5.36 accuracy points in word-level task and 1.44 BLEU in sentence level task. This demonstrates that the initial translation can assist in the generation of both target word and target segment translation. It is worth noting that, after parameters sharing, the improvement in the results using initial translation at the word-level is not obvious. This is because by sharing parameters, our model obtains more generalized encoding results, which reduces the demand for initial translation. Furthermore, in the bi-context type, there is a decrease in accuracy, which may be due to the uncertainty of the correctness of the initial translation.

5.3   Effects of the Length of Human Typed Characters

Furthermore, we conducted experiments to investigate the effect of the length of human typed characters on word-level autocompletion. Figure 5 shows the accuracy achieved with different lengths of human typed characters.

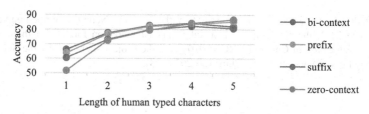

Fig. 5. Accuracy obtained with different length of human typed characters.

We have observed that the accurately is positively correlated with the number of characters typed by human. It can be seen that the accuracy improves with the increase of human typed characters length. This finding is intuitive, as fewer typed characters can lead to more possible choices, particularly when the translation context is restricted or there is no available translation context.

5.4   Effects of the Ratio of Retained Context

We conducted experiments to investigate the effects of the ratio of retained context on word and sentence autocompletion, using the prefix type for convenience. Figure 6 shows the accuracy and TER obtained with different ratio of context.

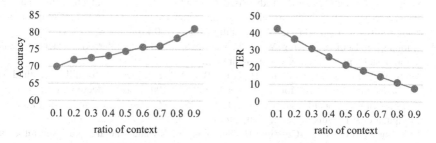

Fig. 6. Accuracy and TER obtained with different ratio of context.

We can see that as the ratio of context increases, the accuracy keeps increasing while the TER score keeps decreasing, indicating that our system can effectively leverage the contextual information to help generate the target word and segment.

6 Conclusion

We propose the WSA method that can not only generate target word but also generate target segment translation in interactive machine translation. The core of WSA is the joint modeling of word and sentence autocomplete tasks through the idea of multi-task learning. We also add information about the initial translation to help autocompletion. Experimental results show that compared with state-of-the-art baselines, our method can significantly improve the accuracy of target word and the quality of target segment translation.

Acknowledgements. This work is supported by the National Natural Science Foundation of China (U1908216), the Humanity and Social Science Foundation for the Youth Scholars of Ministry of Education of China (19YJC740107), and the Project supported by the Science and Technology Plan of Shenyang City, China (20-202-1-28).

References

1. Dzmitry, B., Kyunghyun, C., Yoshua, B.: Neural machine translation by jointly learning to align and translate. In: International Conference on Learning Representations (2014)
2. Vaswani, A., Shazeer, N., Parmar, N., et al.: Attention is all you need. Adv. Neural Inf. Process. Syst. **30**, 5998–6008 (2017)
3. Xiaodong, L., Kevin, D., Liyuan L., Jianfeng, G.: Very deep transformers for neural ma-chine translation. CoRR, abs/2008.07772 (2020)
4. Philippe, L., George, F., Guy, L.: TransType: a computer-aided translation typing system. In: Proceedings of the 2000 NAACL-ANLP Workshop on Embedded machine translation systems, vol. 5, pp. 46–51. Association for Computational Linguistics, USA (2020). https://doi.org/10.3115/1117586.1117593
5. Michel, S., Nicola, U., Pierre, I., Roland, K.: Rule-based translation with statistical phrase-based post-editing. In: Proceedings of the Second Workshop on Statistical Machine Translation, pp. 203–206. Association for Computational Linguistics, USA (2007). https://doi.org/10.5555/1626355.1626383
6. Weijia, X., Marine, C.: Editor: an edit-based transformer with repositioning for neural machine translation with soft lexical constraints. In: Transactions of the Association for Computational Linguistics, vol. 9, pp. 311–328 (2021). https://doi.org/10.1162/tacl_a_00368
7. Guoping, H., Lemao, L., Xing, W., et.al.: TransSmart: A Practical Interactive Machine Translation System, pp. 1–21. arXiv preprint arXiv:2105.13072 (2021)
8. Yanling, X., Lemao, L., Guoping, H., et al.: BiTIIMT: a bilingual text-infilling method for interactive machine translation. In: Proceedings of the 60th Annual Meeting of the Association for Computational Linguistics, vol. 1, pp. 1958–1969. Dublin, Ireland. Association for Computational Linguistics (2022). https://doi.org/10.18653/v1/2022.acl-long.138
9. Huayang, L., Lemao, L., Guoping, H., Shuming, S.: Gwlan: general word-level autocompletion for computer-aided translation. In: Proceedings of the 59th Annual Meeting of the Association for Computational Linguistics and the 11th International Joint Conference on Natural Language Processing, vol. 1, pp. 4792–4802. Online. Association for Computational Linguistics (2021). https://doi.org/10.18653/v1/2021.acl-long.370

10. Sebastin, S., Sandipan, D., Monojit, C., Kalika, B.: INMT: interactive neural machine trans-lation prediction. In: Proceedings of the 2019 Conference on Empirical Methods in Natu-ral Language Processing and the 9th International Joint Conference on Natural Language Pro-cessing (EMNLP-IJCNLP): System Demonstrations, pp. 103–108. Hong Kong, China. Association for Computational Linguistics (2019). https://doi.org/10.18653/v1/D19-3018

11. Guoping, H., Jiajun, Z., Yu, Z., Chengqing, Z.: A new input method for human translators: inte-grating machine translation effectively and imperceptibly. In: International Joint Conference on Artificial Intelligence, pp. 1163–1169 (2015)

12. Melissa, A., Jingshu, L., Jean-gabriel, B., Raheel, Q.: Lingua Custodia's participation at the WMT 2022 word-level auto-completion shared task. In: Proceedings of the Seventh Con-ference on Machine Translation (WMT), pp. 1170–1175, Abu Dhabi, United Arab Emirates (Hybrid). Association for Computational Linguistics (2022)

13. Chris, H., Qun, L.: Lexically constrained decoding for sequence generation using grid beam search. In: Proceedings of the 55th Annual Meeting of the Association for Computational Linguistics, vol. 1, pp. 1535–1546. Vancouver, Canada. Association for Computa-tional Linguistics (2017). https://doi.org/10.18653/v1/P17-1141

14. Matt, P., David, V.: Fast lexically constrained decoding with dynamic beam allocation for neural machine translation. In: Proceedings of the 2018 Conference of the North American Chapter of the Association for Computational Linguistics: Human Language Technologies, vol. 1, pp. 314–1324. New Orleans, Louisiana. Association for Computational Linguistics (2018). https://doi.org/10.18653/v1/N18-1119

15. Rongxiang, W., Hao, Z., Shujian, H., Lei, L., Yifan, X., Jiajun, C.: Correct-and-memorize: learning to translate from interactive revisions. In: Proceedings of the Twenty-Eighth Inter-national Joint Conference on Artificial Intelligence, pp. 5255–5263 (2019). https://doi.org/10.24963/ijcai.2019/730

16. Hendrycks, D., Gimpel, K.: Bridging nonlinearities and stochastic regularizers with gaussian error linear units. In: arXiv preprint arXiv:1606.08415 (2016)

17. Kishore, P., Salim, R., Todd, W., Wei-Jing, Z.: BLEU: a method for automatic evaluation of machine translation. In: Proceedings of the 40th Annual Meeting on Association for Com-putational Linguistics, pp. 311–318. Association for Computational Linguistics, USA (2002). https://doi.org/10.3115/1073083.1073135

ISTIC's Neural Machine Translation Systems for CCMT' 2023

Shuao Guo, Ningyuan Deng, and Yanqing He[✉]

Research Center of Information Theory and Methodology, Institute of Scientific and
Technical Information of China, Beijing 100038, China
{guosa2021,dengny2022,heyq}@istic.ac.cn

Abstract. This paper describes the technical details of ISTIC's
neural machine translation systems for the 19th China Conference
on Machine Translation (CCMT' 2023). ISTIC participated in two
evaluation tasks of machine translation (MT): Low Resource MT
evaluaton task (Vietnamese↔Chinese, Czech↔Chinese, Lao↔Chinese,
Mongolian↔Chinese) and Chinese-Centric Multilingual MT evaluation task (Vietnamese↔Chinese, Thailand↔Chinese, Kazakh↔Chinese,
Hindi↔Chinese, Uyghur↔Chinese). Context-aware systems and a multilingual system are built for two tasks respectively. The paper mainly
illuminates our systems' architecture based on Transformer, data pre-
processing methods and some strategies adopted in these systems. In
addition, the paper evaluates the systems' performance under different
methods.

Keywords: Low resource languages · Multilingual machine
translation · Context-aware

1 Introduction

This paper describes building process and technical details of neural machine
translation (NMT) systems developed by the Institute of Scientific and Technical Information of China (ISTIC) for the 19th China Conference on Machine
Translation (CCMT' 2023). ISTIC participated in two evaluation tasks of
machine translation(MT): Low Resource MT evaluation task and Chinese-
Centric Multilingual MT evaluation task. For Low Resource MT evaluation
task, we built context-aware NMT systems for each of 8 translation directions
(Vietnamese↔Chinese, Czech↔Chinese, Lao↔Chinese, Mongolian↔Chinese).
Contextual information can be incorporated into NMT systems by additional
encoders in context-aware systems. For Chinese-Centric Multilingual MT evaluation task, we built a multilingual NMT system involving five language
pairs and ten translation directions (Vietnamese↔Chinese, Thailand↔Chinese,
Kazakh↔Chinese, Hindi↔Chinese, Uyghur↔Chinese). All systems are built
based on Transformer architecture. Some corpus preprocessing methods are

introduced in this paper. Experiments proved context-aware system can effectively enhance translation quality than baseline system and multilingual MT system has its translation ability over ten translation directions.

2 Data

2.1 Data Size

There are parallel corpus for 8 languages pairs in our NMT systems. All data comes from CCMT2023 evaluation organizer. All systems we submitted belong to constrained systems. Table 1 presents the data size after pre-processing.

Table 1. Data Size

Task	Language pairs	Data size
Chinese-Centric Multilingual MT	Thailand-Chinese(thai-zh)	530K
	Vietnamese-Chinese(vi-zh)	530K
	Uyghur-Chinese(ug-zh)	535K
	Hindi-Chinese(hi-zh)	500K
	Kazakh-Chinese(kk-zh)	475K
Low Resource MT	Vietnamese-Chinese(vi-zh)	196K
	Czech-Chinese(cs-zh)	197K
	Lao-Chinese(lo-zh)	197K
	Mongolian-Chinese(mn-zh)	193K

2.2 Data Preprocessing

As shown in Fig.1, our data preprocessing has four steps, such as character-level preprocessing, tokenization, sentence-level preprocessing and text-level preprocessing.

Character-Level Preprocessing. We filtered special characters such as emoji character, illegal character, the same schedule character to improve data quality [1]. Moses[1] is used to make punctuation normalization and full to half width operations on all characters to achieve format uniformity. Traditional Chinese characters are converted to simplified Chinese characters with python toolkit Hanziconv[2].

---

[1] https://github.com/moses-smt/mosesdecoder.
[2] https://github.com/berniey/hanziconv.

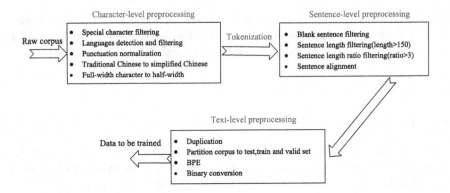

Fig. 1. Preprocessing operations

Tokenization. Multiple tokenization tools are adopted according to different languages including Jieba[3] for Chinese, Underthesea[4] for Vietnam, Pythainlp[5] for Thailand and Lao, Kaznlp[6] for Kazakh, NLTK[7] for Czech and Monparser[8] for Mongolian and Hindi Tokenizer[9] for Hindi. Since words in Uyghur sentences are connected by spaces and there are no appropriate Uyghur tokenization toolkits, we directly consider words connected by spaces in Uyghur sentences as its tokens.

Sentence-Level Preprocessing. We delete language pairs which have at least one blank sentence and use language detection toolkit Py3langid[10] to detect language pairs which don't meet language requirements and delete them. After that, we delete the language pairs whose sentence length is greater than 150 and sentence length ratio is greater than 3.

Text-Level Preprocessing. Firstly we remove duplicated sentence pairs for each language direction and split the data into validation set, test set and training set. Then we learn Byte-Pair Encoding(BPE) [2] for each language in Low Resource MT evaluation task and a joint BPE over all languages involved in Chinese-Centric Multilingual MT evaluation task. BPE merge operations in two tasks are both 32K. At last we converse data to binary fomat with fairseq-preprocess[11].

---

[3] https://github.com/fxsjy/jieba.

[4] https://github.com/undertheseanlp/underthesea.

[5] https://github.com/PyThaiNLP/pythainlp.

[6] https://github.com/nlacslab/kaznlp.

[7] https://www.nltk.org/.

[8] https://github.com/realzoberg/Mon-Parser.

[9] https://github.com/sheoguo/hinditokenizer.

[10] https://github.com/adbar/py3langid.

[11] https://github.com/facebookresearch/fairseq.

3   System

All systems we built for the two tasks are all based on standard Transformer [3]. Standard Transformer is an Encoder-Decoder structure(see Fig.2), which has 12 blocks containing 6 layers stacked encoders and 6 layers stacked decoders. Model dimension is 521, the number of attention head in every encoder and every decoder is 8, the dimension of feed forward network in every encoder and every decoder is 2048.

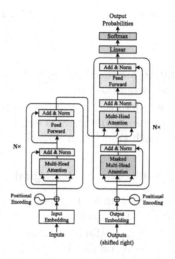

Fig. 2. Transformer architecture

3.1   Systems for Low Resource MT Evaluation Task

We built 8 NMT systems according to 8 translation directions specified by Low Resource MT task. They are Vietnamese -to-Chinese NMT system, Lao-to-Chinese NMT system, Mongolian-to-Chinese NMT system, Czech-to-Chinese NMT system, Chinese-to-Vietnamese NMT system, Chinese-to-Lao NMT system, Chinese-to-Mongolian NMT system and Chinese-to-Czech NMT system respectively. All systems in this task are context-aware NMT systems with multi encoders based on Transformer-base architecture.

Context-aware NMT is a model to incorporate contextual information into NMT [4]. In this model multi-encoder can take the surrounding sentences as the context and encode them by an additional neural networks. There are two methods of integrating the context into NMT, they are outside integration [5] and inside integration [6]. For outside integration, as Fig. 3 shows, the representations of the context and the current sentence are firstly transformed into a new representation by an attention network. Then the attention output and the

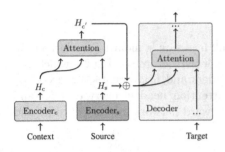
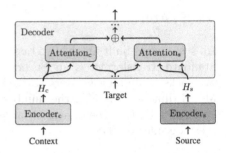

Fig. 3. Outside integration   **Fig. 4.** Inside Integration

source sentence representation are fused by a gated sum. For inside integration, as Fig. 4 shows, decoder can attend to two encoders respectively. Then, the gating mechanism inside the decoder is employed to obtain the fusion vector. In our experiments, the context we use to integrate is source language sentences from corresponding train set for each translation direction.

3.2 System for Chinese-Centric Multilingual MT Evaluation Task

We built a multilingual NMT system for Chinese-Centric Multilingual MT evaluaton task. The multilingual NMT model uses a shared encoder and a shared decoder for Vietnamese, Thailand, Hindi, Kazakh, Uyghur and Chinese. The whole multilingual system is based on multilingual Transformer (mTransformer) [7]. mTransformer has the same encoder-decoder architecture as standard Tranformer but instead introduces an language identifying token at the beginning of the input sentence(See Fig. 5). The language identifying token is a label used to represent the language of the sentences in train set.

Define our system's multilingual dataset [8]:

$$D_{multi} = \{D_{src \rightarrow zh}, D_{zh \rightarrow tgt}\}, src, tgt \in \{vi, ug, hi, thai, kk\}$$

We train our multilingual MT model with the following loss:

$$\ell = \sum_{d \in D_{multi}} \sum_{<x,y> \in d} - \log P_\theta(y|x)$$

where d is dataset for each language pair in D_{multi}, $<x, y>$ is a sentence pair from s_i to t_i in dataset d, and θ is the model parameter.

Source sentence: __zh__ 他 比 他 的 同学 刻苦 一些 。
Target sentence: __kk__ Ол сыныптастарынан гөрі көп жұмыс істейді .

Source sentence: __zh__ 可是 他 一毛钱 没找 我 拿 。
Target sentence: __thai__ แต่ว่า เขา ไม่ ได้ ขอ เงิน ผม แม้ แต่ สตางค์แดง เดียว

Fig. 5. Sentence examples for lanuage identifying token

4 Experiments

4.1 System Environment

Context-aware NMT system and multilingual NMT system are trained in different training environments. Tables 3 shows systems's environment settings.

Table 2. Environment settings

	Context-aware NMT system	Multilingual NMT system
DL framework	Pytorch 1.5.0	Pytorch 1.8.0
NMT framework	Fairseq 0.6.0	Fairseq 0.10.0
Number of GPU	4	8
OS	CentOS Linux release 7.6.1810 (Core)	
GPU	NVIDIA TITAN Xp(12GB)	

4.2 Model and Train

A baseline system and a context-aware system are trained for every translation direction in Low Resourece MT evaluation task. Standard Transformer architecture is used to train baseline system and context-aware system is trained by both inside and outside integration methods. The trained data of source language in every translation direction is copied as contextual information incorporated into corresponding context-aware system. Every model was optimized with Adam [9] with an initial learning rate of 0.0001, which was multiplied by 0.7 whenever perplexity on the validation set was not improved for three checkpoints. When it was not improved for eight checkpoints, we stopped the training. Dropout probabilities is set to 0.3, the loss function is set to "label smoothed cross entropy" and warm-up steps are set to 4000. Beam search [10] is adopted in decoding stage.

Considering the diversity of dataset volume, transformer_iswlt_de_en architecture is used to train the multilingual NMT system. This architecture belongs to variants of Transformer architecture, the number of attention head in every encoder and every decoder is 4, the dimension of feed forward network in every encoder and every decoder is 1024. The method of temperature sampling is used in model training and sampling_temperature is 4. Other model parameter settings and training process are the same as systems in Low Resource MT evaluation task.

4.3 Experiments Results

We use character BLEU [11] to evaluate translation quality with sacrebleu[12].Table 3 shows the NMT systems' BLEU in Low resource MT evaluation

---

[12] https://github.com/mjpost/sacrebleu.

task. Table 4 shows multilingual system's BLEU in Chinese-Centric Multilingual MT evaluation task.

Table 3. BLEU for systems in Low resource MT task

	Baseline	Inside integration	Outside integration
cs → zh	33.93	34.03	34.11
lo → zh	26.70	26.97	26.83
mn → zh	21.34	21.78	22.09
vi → zh	28.59	28.56	28.86
zh → cs	26.00	27.01	26.83
zh → lo	11.85	12.76	13.01
zh → mn	29.44	30.55	30.42
zh → vi	26.94	27.40	27.53

Table 4. BLEU for the multilingual system

Translation direction	BLEU
kk → zh	33.93
thai → zh	26.70
vi → zh	21.34
ug → zh	28.59
hi → zh	26.00
zh → kk	11.85
zh → thai	29.44
zh → vi	26.94
zh → ug	26.94
zh → hi	26.94

As shown in Table 3, no matter inside integration or outside integration, context-aware system's performance is prior to baseline system in 8 translation directions. So we believe context-aware system can enhance the model's performance effectively. The best performance system for every translation direction is choosed to submit to evaluation organizer. As shown in Table 4, our multilingual MT system demonstrates its translation ability over ten translation directions. We submitted this multilingual MT system to evaluation organizer.

5   Conclusion

In this paper, we describe building process and technical details of translation systems for Low Resource MT evaluation task and Chinese-Centric Multilingual MT evaluation task. In Low Resource MT evaluation task, we construct context-aware system for eight translation directions and our experiments proved context-aware system can effectively enhance translation quality. In Chinese-Centric Multilingual MT evaluation task, we trained a multilingual NMT system with ten translation directions. Experiments proved this multilingual MT system has its translation ability over ten translation directions, but there are imbalance in translation abilities among different language pairs.

Due to the time constraint, we didn't attempt to use LLM pre-training models approaches to enhance NMT model performance. In the future we will further explore such approaches for these two tasks.

Acknowledgement. The work is supported by the Key Project of Institute of Scientific and Technical Information of China (Grant No.ZD2023-11).

References

1. Guo, S., Guo, H., He, Y., Lan, T.: ISTIC's Thai-to-Chinese neural machine translation system for CCMT 2022. In: Xiao, T., Pino, J. (eds) Machine Translation. CCMT 2022. Communications in Computer and Information Science, vol. 1671. Springer, Singapore (2022). https://doi.org/10.1007/978-981-19-7960-6_16

2. Sennrich, R., Haddow, B., Birch, A.: Neural machine translation of rare words with subword units. In: Proceedings of the 54th Annual Meeting of the Association for Computational Linguistics (Volume 1: Long Papers), Berlin, Germany, pp. 1715–1725. Association for Computational Linguistics (2016)

3. Vaswani, A., et al.: Attention is all you need. In: Advances In Neural Information Processing Systems 30 (NIPS 2017), pp. 5998–6008. Neural Information Processing Systems, Online (2017)

4. Li, B., et al.: Does multi-encoder help? a case study on context-aware neural machine translation. In: Proceedings of the 58th Annual Meeting of the Association for Computational Linguistics, pp. 3512–3518. Association for Computational Linguistics, Online (2020)

5. Zhang, J.: Improving the transformer translation model with document-level context. In: Proceedings of the 2018 Conference on Empirical Methods in Natural Language Processing, Brussels, Belgium, pp. 533–542. Association for Computational Linguistics (2018)

6. Voita, E., et al.: Context-aware neural machine translation learns anaphora resolution. In: Proceedings of the 56th Annual Meeting of the Association for Computational Linguistics, pp. 1264–1274. Association for Computational Linguistics, Online (2018)

7. Johnson, M., et al.: Google's multilingual neural machine translation system: enabling zero-shot translation. Trans. Assoc. Comput. Lingu. **5**, 339–351 (2017)

8. Lin, Z., Wu, L., Wang, M., Li, L.: Learning language specific sub-network for multilingual machine translation. In: Proceedings of the 59th Annual Meeting of the Association for Computational Linguistics and the 11th International Joint Conference on Natural Language Processing (Volume 1: Long Papers), pp. 293–305, Online. Association for Computational Linguistics (2021)
9. Kingma, D.P., Ba, J.: Adam: A Method for Stochastic Optimization. CoRR abs/ arXiv: 1412.6980 (2014)
10. Vijayakumar, A.K., et al.: Diverse Beam Search: Decoding Diverse Solutions from Neural Sequence Models (2016)
11. Papineni, K., Roukos, S., Ward, T., Zhu, W.-J.: Bleu: a method for automatic evaluation of machine translation. In: Proceedings of the 40th Annual Meeting of the Association for Computational Linguistics, Philadelphia, Pennsylvania, USA, pp. 311–318. Association for Computational Linguistics (2002)

A Novel Dataset and Benchmark Analysis on Document Image Translation

Zhiyang Zhang[1,2], Yaping Zhang[1,2], Lu Xiang[1,2], Yang Zhao[1,2], Yu Zhou[1,3], and Chengqing Zong[1,2(✉)]

[1] State Key Laboratory of Multimodal Artificial Intelligence Systems (MAIS), Institute of Automation, Chinese Academy of Sciences, Beijing, China
`zhangzhiyang2020@ia.ac.cn,`
`{yaping.zhang,lu.xiang,yang.zhao,yzhou,cqzong}@nlpr.ia.ac.cn`
[2] School of Artificial Intelligence, University of Chinese Academy of Sciences, Beijing, China
[3] Fanyu AI Laboratory, Zhongke Fanyu Technology Co., Ltd., Beijing, China

Abstract. Document image translation (DIT) deserves more attention on account of its importance in many real-world scenarios. It is a challenging task because of the *layout degeneration* and *noisy text translation* problems caused by the optical character recognition (OCR) model. Moreover, due to the task-specific annotation, existing document image datasets usually do not support in-depth DIT analysis and model development. So, to motivate a broader investigation, this paper presents a dataset named *DITrans*, which provides fine-grained annotations for English-to-Chinese DIT task. It contains 2.8k English document images in three domains: *political report*, *scientific article* and *paper book*. Each document image has been annotated with *layout structure*, *source text* and *translation references*. Based on *DITrans*, a novel framework, which strengthens the conventional OCR-Translation cascade in *layout awareness* and *noise robustness* for better DIT, has been proposed. Furthermore, benchmark evaluations and detailed analysis based on this framework have been conducted. The evaluations and analysis results demonstrate that the dataset is very practical and can facilitate full-stack analysis and long-term research on DIT.

Keywords: Document image translation · New dataset · Benchmark · OCR · Layout structure

1 Introduction

Document image translation (DIT), aiming to perform language translation from scanned/camera document images with complex visual and layout formats, is critical for many practical applications such as translating ancient books, scientific articles and webpage screenshots, *etc.*

© The Author(s), under exclusive license to Springer Nature Singapore Pte Ltd. 2023
Y. Feng and C. Feng (Eds.): CCMT 2023, CCIS 1922, pp. 103–115, 2023.
https://doi.org/10.1007/978-981-99-7894-6_10

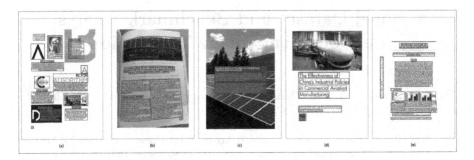

Fig. 1. *DITrans* samples. Document images are of various layouts and visual elements (glyphs, word arts, embedded figures, *etc*). Source text fragment boxes are shown in cyan. Layout blocks are shown in red. Other annotations (logical order, translation references, *etc*) are not visualized to avoid overcrowding. (Color figure online)

However, the existing method of directly joining the separately optimized optical character recognition (OCR) model and machine translation (MT) model cannot achieve optimal DIT, because of the following two problems.

– **Layout degeneration.** After being processed by OCR parser, a document image loses its layout structure and logical order, degenerating into a batch of unordered, semantically truncated text fragments. *E.g.*, the text fragments enveloped by cyan boxes in Fig. 1.
– **Noisy text translation.** The OCR output is noise-contaminated text instead of clean text as in the training phase of the MT model.

Such problems burden the translation process, making DIT much more challenging than plain text MT. Therefore, we claim the two capabilities that a superior DIT model should possess - the awareness of layout structure and the robustness to OCR noise. Nevertheless, existing document image datasets [3,6,8–11,15–18] may not support the development of such models and in-depth analysis for DIT, because their monotonic annotation is targeted for individual tasks (*i.e.*, layout analysis, logical order detection, OCR), instead of the comprehensive DIT. Therefore, to facilitate long-term research on DIT, it is inevitable to create a real-world dataset with fine-grained annotations, which support the detailed analysis of all intermediate sub-modules and innovative attempts such as layout structure utilization, OCR noise reduction, *etc*.

To this end, we have developed a novel dataset named *DITrans*, which is characterized by multiple domains and fine-grained annotations for English-to-Chinese DIT. It contains both synthetic and human-annotated high-quality annotations for document images in three domains: *political report, scientific article* and *paper book* (Fig. 1). Each document image has been annotated with *layout structure, source text* and *translation references* (Fig. 2). With these fine-grained annotations, *DITrans* is suitable for multiple document image tasks, including layout analysis, logical order detection, OCR and DIT.

Based on *DITrans*, we have developed a novel DIT framework. It is based on the conventional OCR-MT cascade and is strengthened in two aspects: 1) For **layout degeneration** problem, an additional layout analysis module is integrated with our layout-aware aggregation strategy to make the whole system aware of layout structure and logical order. 2) For **noisy text translation** problem, the pre-trained translation module is further enhanced with our modified adversarial stability fine-tuning strategy to be robust to OCR noise. Based on this framework, benchmark evaluations of various system variants are explored extensively. Furthermore, detailed analysis of the **layout structure** and **OCR noise** has been conducted. The discovery is very inspiring for new methodologies. In summary, our contributions are three-fold:

- A new dataset for English-to-Chinese DIT has been constructed. It provides fine-grained annotations including *layout structure, source text* and *translation references* for 2.8k document images in three domains.
- A novel DIT framework has been proposed and the performances of different system variants have been benchmarked.
- The impact of layout structure and OCR noise on DIT has been carefully studied to enlighten the proposal of new methodologies.

2   DITrans

In this section, we first give a detailed introduction to *DITrans*' fine-grained annotations and then give a cursory review of its construction workflow.

2.1   Fine-Grained Annotations

As shown in Fig. 2, the annotations can be represented as a triplet (*layout structure, source text, translation references*). Each element contains more fine-grained annotations described below.

Layout Structure. A document image is composed of multiple layout blocks (paragraph, table, figure, etc.) in a certain layout and logical order (Fig. 2 (a)). In *DITrans*, each layout block is annotated with *layout id, layout attribution* and *layout box*, as shown in Fig. 2 (b). With annotations of layout structure, *DITrans* is suitable for tasks including physical layout analysis and logical order detection.

- *Layout id.* It gives the logical order of a layout block. *E.g.*, A *layout id* of *4* represents the fourth reading object according to human reading order.
- *Layout attribution.* It gives a semantic label to each layout block. 14 semantic labels are defined for *DITrans*: {author-info, caption, math, image, header, footer, footnote, page-number, list-label, paragraph, reference, heading, table and unknown}.
- *Layout box.* It indicates the position of a layout block. Specifically, each layout block is enveloped by a rectangular box, with the coordinates of its upper left vertex (x_ul, y_ul) and lower right vertex (x_lr, y_lr) extracted.

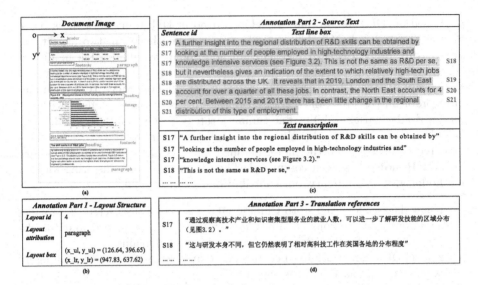

Fig. 2. An annotation example of *DITrans*. The annotation is represented as a triplet (*layout structure, source text, translation references*). Each element contains more fine-grained annotations. (a) Document image. The bounding boxes in green and blue wrap the objects to be annotated. For brevity, here we only present the fine-grained annotations for the blue box in (b) (c) and (d). (b) *Layout structure*, including *layout id, layout attribution* and *layout box*. (c) *Source text*, including *sentence id, text line box* and *transcription* of each source text fragment. (d) Chinese *translation references*, annotated at sentence level. (Color figure online)

Source Text. Source text contains *sentence id, text line box* and *text transcription* as shown in Fig. 2 (c).

- *Sentence id.* It indicates the reading order of a sentence. For cross-line sentences, we annotate their text fragments line by line and assign the same *sentence id* to these text fragments (Fig. 2 (c) top).
- *Text line box.* It indicates the position of a sentence. Each text fragment is enveloped by a rectangular box and the coordinates of this box are extracted to be the text line box.
- *Text transcription.* Text transcription is also annotated fragment by fragment (Fig. 2 (c) bottom), and each transcribed text fragment is aligned with its corresponding *sentence id* and *text line box*.

Translation References. As shown in Fig. 2 (d), the Chinese translation of each source sentence is given.

2.2   Dataset Construction

DITrans is composed of human-annotated data and synthetic data. The former is of high quality and the latter can be leveraged as augmented data to further improve model performance.

Human-annotated data includes three domains: *political report*, *scientific article* and *paper book*. Each domain corresponds to a unique data source: 1) *Political reports* are from the British Government Report Collection[1] and amount to 1,397 pages of 5 topics including economy, education, environment, health and technology. 2) *Scientific articles* are from arXiv and amount to 117 pages of 3 topics including machine learning, computer vision and natural language processing. 3) *Paper books* amount to 137 pages of 2 topics including opinion reviews and instructional notes. Then, the collected political reports and scientific articles were scanned and paper books were photographed for the next human annotation process. We hired 35 professional annotators for layout structure and source text and 33 translators for document translation. Translators were shown a document image with layout and source text and were required to produce correct and fluent translations in Chinese. For quality control, We hired 8 professional annotators to sample and check the annotated instances.

To further enrich *DITrans* with **synthetic data**, we automatically synthesized the complete annotations for 1,170 document images from DocBank [8]. First, we retrieved 1,170 document images belonging to the computer science domain with keyword-matching heuristics and further human inspection. Second, for each document image, words belonging to the same layout block were aggregated into a text block and segmented into sentences with an unsupervised segmentation algorithm.[2] Then, the *text line boxes* were obtained by merging adjacent word boxes. After reordering the layout blocks with the reading flow algorithm [12], the layout structure and source text annotations were produced. Finally, a commercial machine translation tool[3] was employed for sentence-level translation. This workflow extended *DITrans* with 1,170 *scientific article* document images. This part of data is referred to as *DocImg-syn*.

2.3   Dataset Statistics and Comparison

We compare *DITrans* with other widely-used document image datasets in Table 1. Statistics of *DITrans* are shown in Table 2. The two unique features of our dataset are summarized as follows.

- *Realistic and Multi-domain*. Three domains of document images are provided, whose acquisition approaches are scanning and photographing - two common ways to obtain document images in real-world scenarios.
- *Fine-Grained Annotations*. Fine-grained annotations are provided to make *DITrans* applicable for multiple document image tasks, such as DIT, OCR, layout analysis, logical order detection, etc.

---

[1] https://www.gov.uk/.
[2] http://www.nltk.org/api/nltk.tokenize.html.
[3] https://fanyi-api.baidu.com/.

Table 1. Comparison between *DITrans* and some existing document image datasets.

Dataset	Annotation	# Pages	Domain	Acquisition	Layout Block Order	Layout Box	Layout Attribution	Source Text Transcription	Translation References
PubLayNet(Zhong et al. [18])	automatic	360k	scientific article	converted from PDF		✓	✓		
DocBank(Li et al. [8])	automatic	500k	scientific article	converted from PDF		✓	✓	✓	
ReadingBank(Wang et al. [15])	automatic	500k	scientific article	converted from WORD	✓			✓	
PRImA(Antonacopoulos et al. [1])	manual	1.2k	magazine, technical article	scanning		✓	✓		
DITrans	manual & automatic	2.8k	political report, scientific article, paper book	scanning & photographing	✓	✓	✓	✓	✓

Table 2. Statistics of *DITrans*.

Domain	Annotation	# Pages	# Layout Blocks	# Source Sentences	# Words	Average #Words in Each Layout Block	Average #Words of Each Source Sentence	Average #Words of Each Translation Reference
Political Report	Human-annotated	1,397	11,980	37,691	599,000	49.82	21.43	20.91
Scientific Article	Human-annotated	117	1,357	3,978	94,990	69.25	18.93	22.03
Paper Book	Human-annotated	137	1,096	2,887	62,472	56.83	20.26	20.18
DocImg-syn	Synthetic	1,170	11,048	36,212	718,120	65.25	17.04	17.19

3 Benchmark

3.1 Layout-Aware Robust DIT Framework

The DIT task is defined as generating the translated document in logical order for a given document image. In this section, we introduce our novel layout-aware robust DIT framework - LARDIT (Fig. 3), composed of three working stages described in detail below.

Stage 1: Text Extraction and Layout Analysis. *1) Text extraction* aims at extracting the source text from a given document image I. Specifically, an OCR parser is applied on I with the resulting text fragments $F = \{f_1, f_2, ..., f_n\}$, which is typically organized in rule-based order (*e.g.*, from top to bottom). F can be further decomposed into OCR fragments text $F^{text} = \{f_1^{text}, f_2^{text}, ..., f_n^{text}\}$ and OCR fragments position $F^{pos} = \{f_1^{pos}, f_2^{pos}, ..., f_n^{pos}\}$. *2) Layout analysis* aims at parsing the layout structure from I both physically and logically, making layout blocks first detected and then arranged in logical order. **i) Physical layout analysis** returns a sequence of detected layout blocks $B' = \{b_1', b_2', ..., b_m'\}$ from I. For each layout block b_i', it determines its category label $b_i'^{ctg}$, its bounding box position $b_i'^{pos}$, and the confidence score $b_i'^{cfd}$. **ii) Logical order detection** employs the reading flow algorithm [12] to arrange the detected layout blocks B' into $B = \{b_1, b_2, ..., b_m\}$ with logical order instead of the original descending order of confidence score.

Stage 2: Layout-Aware Aggregation. With the extracted text fragments and layout structure, a novel mapping strategy is proposed to aggregate the text semantics $F = \{f_1, f_2, ..., f_n\}$ and visual layout $B^{pos} = \{b_1^{pos}, b_2^{pos}, ..., b_m^{pos}\}$

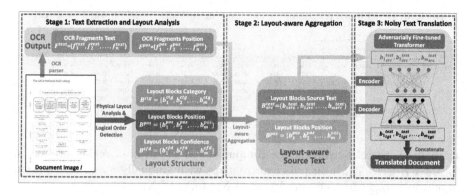

Fig. 3. Schematic diagram of our DIT framework LARDIT.

to form the well-ordered source text blocks $B_{src}^{text} = \{b_{1\ src}^{text}, b_{2\ src}^{text}, ..., b_{m\ src}^{text}\}$. Specifically, for the i_{th} element of B_{src}^{text}:

$$b_{i\ src}^{text} = concat(f_j^{text} | f_j^{pos} \in b_i^{pos}), \qquad (1)$$

where $concat(\cdot)$ denotes the concatenation of text fragments from top to bottom according to their y coordinates.

Stage 3: Noisy Text Translation. To alleviate the OCR noise problem, the adversarial stability fine-tuning strategy [2] is first modified to adapt to our task and then leveraged to fine-tune the pre-trained machine translation model for better tolerance to OCR noise. The core idea is to improve the robustness of both the encoder and decoder of translation model. To this end, during the training phase, the encoder is encouraged to output similar intermediate representations for both the original and adversarial input; The decoder is guided to generate the correct output given the adversarial input or original input. In our modification, instead of manually constructing the pseudo adversarial input, which may have a distribution gap from the real-world noise, we directly treat the OCR noisy text as adversarial input. During the test phase, source text blocks in $B_{src}^{text} = \{b_{1\ src}^{text}, b_{2\ src}^{text}, ..., b_{m\ src}^{text}\}$ are sequentially translated into target text blocks $B_{tgt}^{text} = \{b_{1\ tgt}^{text}, b_{2\ tgt}^{text}, ..., b_{m\ tgt}^{text}\}$ and are finally concatenated to form a well-ordered translated document.

3.2   System Variants

We have evaluated diverse system variants based on LARDIT, each composed of different module combinations as described below.

Layout Analysis Module Variants. We build upon object detection models for physical layout analysis. Two popular object detection networks are experimented with. *a) Faster R-CNN* [13]. Its Region Proposal Network (RPN) shares the convolutional feature map with the detection network through attention

Table 3. Benchmark results of various system variants based on our framework.

System Variants		Evaluation Results											
Layout Analysis Module	TranslationModule	Political Report				Scientific Article				Paper Book			
		BLEU↑	ROUGE-2↑	ROUGE-L↑	METEOR↑	BLEU↑	ROUGE-2↑	ROUGE-L↑	METEOR↑	BLEU↑	ROUGE-2↑	ROUGE-L↑	METEOR↑
Faster R-CNN	Transformer-PT	16.27	13.73	29.39	36.45	8.58	17.65	30.50	25.34	11.45	7.95	18.04	30.35
	Transformer-FT	23.58	15.49	33.35	44.65	16.16	19.19	33.27	34.51	13.63	9.34	23.83	33.49
	Transformer-ASF	27.41	35.78	55.25	49.17	22.01	34.48	50.22	40.28	15.87	13.32	31.65	39.12
Mask R-CNN	Transformer-PT	16.05	13.24	28.51	35.88	8.15	17.47	30.67	24.81	11.30	7.68	18.09	29.43
	Transformer-FT	23.36	16.56	33.92	43.87	16.38	18.85	33.21	34.47	13.14	9.12	22.01	33.96
	Transformer-ASF	**30.38**	**41.72**	**59.86**	**51.08**	**22.81**	**42.37**	**56.11**	**41.05**	**19.91**	**15.23**	**38.62**	**40.10**

mechanism, thereby reducing the computational overhead of region proposals. *b) Mask R-CNN* [5]. It outputs feature maps with gradually reduced resolution in multiple stages to a Feature Pyramid Network (FPN).

Translation Module Variants. Three translation models based on Transformer [14] are experimented with. *a) Transformer-PT*. Transformer-base that is pre-trained on WMT22 en-zh bilingual parallel corpus. *b) Transformer-FT*. Transformer-PT is further fine-tuned on our *DITrans* training set. *c) Transformer-ASF*. Transformer-PT is further fine-tuned on *DITrans* training set with our modified adversarial stability fine-tuning strategy.

3.3   Benchmark Results

Benchmark results are shown in Table 3. **First**, the combination of {Mask R-CNN + Transformer-ASF} is the best-performing system. Faster R-CNN and Mask R-CNN perform at roughly the same level if combined with Transformer-PT/FT. **Second**, fine-tuning the translation module improves the performance of all three domains by a large margin. This indicates a domain difference between *DITrans* and WMT22 news corpus, and fine-tuning mitigates the domain inconsistency. **Third**, our modified adversarial stability fine-tuning strategy significantly improves the translation for all three domains, demonstrating its effectiveness in addressing OCR noise.

4   Analysis

In this section, we conduct detailed analysis from perspectives of **OCR noise** and **layout structure** to enlighten new methodologies for DIT's **noisy text translation** and **layout degeneration** problems.

4.1   Analysis of OCR Noise

Overall Impact. As shown in Table 4, DIT falls behind the plain text translation of ground truth with a large margin for all three domains: 11.51, 11.11 and 9.31 BLEU declines for *political report, scientific article* and *paper book*, respectively. The main reason lies in the OCR noise, which causes a distribution shift to the translation module from clean text during training to noisy text during testing.

Table 4. Comparison between translating the OCR noisy source text and translating ground truth clean source text.

Noisy Text or Ground Truth	Political Report				Scientific Article				Paper Book			
	BLEU↑	ROUGE-2↑	ROUGE-L↑	METEOR↑	BLEU↑	ROUGE-2↑	ROUGE-L↑	METEOR↑	BLEU↑	ROUGE-2↑	ROUGE-L↑	METEOR↑
Faster R-CNN + OCR noisy text + Transformer-FT	23.58	15.49	33.35	44.65	16.16	19.19	33.27	34.51	13.63	9.34	23.83	33.49
Faster R-CNN + ground truth + Transformer-FT	35.09	48.20	63.98	56.26	27.27	46.75	59.89	46.00	22.94	22.71	51.33	45.83

Table 5. CER of OCR and its impact on translation. BLEU_GT and BLEU_OCR correspond to ground truth translation and OCR noisy sentence translation, respectively.

	CER↓	BLEU_GT↑	BLEU_OCR↑	Δ BLEU
Political Report	13.82%	39.5	24.9	14.6
Scientific Article	19.04%	30.7	16.4	14.3

Detailed Analysis. We further set a simplified version of the DIT task by shielding other variables (layout, sentence segmentation, *etc.*) to concentrate on the sentence-level fine-grained analysis of OCR noise. Specifically, we extract each sentence's image patch with the gold-standard line box and apply the OCR-MT procedure to get its noisy source sentence and translation.

First, the OCR character error rate (CER) and BLEU decline caused by OCR noise are shown in Table 5. *The CER of political report and scientific article are 13.82% and 19.04%, respectively, resulting in a serious BLEU decline of 14.6 and 14.3.* Second, the average ΔBLEU within different CER intervals is given in Table 6. The average ΔBLEU is the sum of the BLEU decline of each sentence divided by the total # sentences within the given CER interval. It measures the impact of OCR noise at different levels on the translation quality. As shown in Table 6, sentences within [0, 1%] CER interval can be regarded as clean texts so that the translation quality remains almost unchanged. However, such sentences only account for 2.9% for *political report* and 1.4% for *scientific article*. CER of most sentences exceeds 1%. Moreover, *with the increase of CER, the BLEU decreases more severely, showing the vulnerability of the translation module to OCR noise.*

Challenges in Addressing OCR Noise. Three methods for OCR noise are experimented with. *1) Noisy text fine-tuning*: The translation module is fine-tuned with the OCR noisy text-reference bi-text to be adapted to OCR noise. *2) Post-correction*: An additional error corrector, BertChecker [7], is employed for OCR error correction. *3) Adversarial fine-tuning*: The translation module is fine-tuned with the original-adversarial sample pairs for better tolerance to OCR noise.

Table 6. Impact of OCR noise on translation within different CER intervals.

#	CER	Political Report			Scientific Article		
		# Sen	Percentage of # Sen	Avg. ΔBLEU	# Sen	Percentage of # Sen	Avg. ΔBLEU
1	[0, 1%]	117	2.9%	1.59	122	1.4%	0.45
2	(1%, 5%]	518	12.9%	8.51	490	5.7%	6.33
3	(5%, 10%]	797	19.9%	13.76	1064	12.4%	10.41
4	(10%, 20%]	645	16.1%	19.24	1340	15.6%	13.22
5	(20%, 30%]	192	4.8%	24.64	523	6.1%	12.76
6	(30%, 100%]	1738	43.4%	26.81	5060	58.8%	18.42
Total	[0, 100%]	4007	100%	19.79	8599	100%	15.33

Table 7. Performance of methods to address OCR noise. Metric is BLEU.

Methods to Address OCR Noise	OCR Noisy Source Sentence		Ground Truth Source Sentence	
	Political Report	Scientific Article	Political Report	Scientific Article
None	24.9	16.4	39.5	30.7
Noisy Text Fine-tuning	26.5 (+1.6)	17.1 (+0.7)	37.6 (−1.9)	27.7 (−3.0)
Post-correction	26.0 (+1.1)	16.8 (+0.4)	38.8 (−0.7)	29.9 (−0.8)
Adversarial Fine-tuning	27.2 (+2.3)	18.2 (+1.8)	32.9 (−6.6)	25.3 (−5.4)

As shown in Table 7, *all three methods improve BLEU, among which adversarial fine-tuning performs the best.* However, they still suffer from: 1) The deficiency which results in a large margin compared with the ground truth translation. 2) The ability degradation of clean sentence translation. Therefore, *a more balanced scheme that resists OCR noise without sacrificing the capacity to translate clean sentences, deserves further exploration.* One feasible direction is to leverage the sentence image patch for auxiliary cross-modal features.

4.2   Analysis of Layout Structure

Overall Impact. The layout degeneration problem caused by the OCR module brings two issues: 1) Truncated text fragments instead of complete sentences are transcribed. 2) The disordered arrangement of these text fragments. Such issues lead to cluttered, semantically confused source text and finally a poorly document translation. As shown in Table 8, the removal of layout analysis module leads to 11.11, 11.59 and 2.97 BLEU decline for *political report, scientific article*, and *paper book*, respectively, *demonstrating the indispensability of layout structure incorporation for DIT.*

Detailed Analysis. For detailed analysis, gold-standard line box and transcribed text are employed as "perfect" OCR output to shield the impact of OCR noise. The {validation set + test set} of *political report* are divided into two parts according to layout complexity: 1) Regular-layout document images with rectangular layout blocks in single column (Fig. 1 (c)(d)). 2) Irregular-layout document images with layout blocks in multiple columns or even scattered distribution (Fig. 1 (a)). Two methods are compared under this setting. *1) Base*: Layout structure is completely disregarded, *i.e.*, the transcribed text is

Table 8. Comparison between systems with/without layout analysis module.

With or Without Layout Analysis Module	Political Report				Scientific Article				Paper Book			
	BLEU↑	ROUGE-2↑	ROUGE-L↑	METEOR↑	BLEU↑	ROUGE-2↑	ROUGE-L↑	METEOR↑	BLEU↑	ROUGE-2↑	ROUGE-L↑	METEOR↑
Faster R-CNN + Transformer-FT	**23.58**	**15.49**	**33.35**	**44.65**	**16.16**	**19.19**	**33.27**	**34.51**	**13.63**	**9.34**	**23.83**	**33.49**
- Faster R-CNN	12.47	9.40	22.51	33.46	4.57	6.89	19.88	19.77	10.66	8.31	22.24	31.30

Table 9. Performance comparison between method without layout and method with gold-standard layout. Evaluation metric is BLEU.

Layout Category	Regular-layout	Irregular-layout
# pages	141	139
Base	35.6	28.9
Gold-standard Layout	43.6	39.7
Δ BLEU	8.0	10.8

translated fragment by fragment and is arranged from top to bottom. *2) Gold-standard layout*: Text fragments are aggregated with the gold-standard layout box and are arranged in annotated logical order. Then, sentence segmentation and translation are performed for each text block.

As shown in Table 9, *for regular/irregular document images, the aggregation of layout structure improves BLEU by 8.0 and 10.8, respectively.* The more fine-grained BLEU improvement concerning document image proportion is shown in Fig. 4. ΔBLEU is less than 16 for 90.10% regular-layout document images. While irregular-layout document images with ΔBLEU ≥ 16 still account for 26.60%, indicating that *the translation improvement may be greater for irregular-layout document images.*

Challenges in Leveraging Layout. Three typical layout analysis approaches are experimented with. *1) Rule-based*: The rule-based reading flow algorithm [12], sentence segmentation and translation are applied to text fragments sequentially. *2) Projection-based*: Recursive X-Y cut [4] is employed to decompose a document image recursively into a set of rectangular layout blocks. *3) Object Detection-based*: Object detection neural network (Faster R-CNN) is used for layout block detection.

Based on Table 10, the following conclusions could be reached. 1) For regular-layout document images, the rule-based method works as well as the gold-standard layout. For irregular-layout document images, the object detection-based method performs best and reaches the same level as gold-standard layout, beating the rule-based and projection-based methods by a large margin. 2) Despite the performance superiority, the object detection-based method suffers inferior inference time - 3.5 times that of the translation module. Therefore, *for irregular-layout document images, how to make time-efficient use of layout structure, deserves further investigation.* One feasible direction is to mine the semantics and position of OCR text fragments for simultaneous layout analysis and translation instead of the current cascaded, two-stage approach.

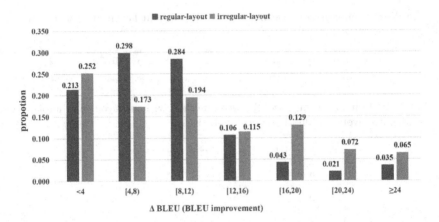

Fig. 4. Proportion of document images within different ΔBLEU intervals.

Table 10. Performance of methods of leveraging layout structure. The evaluation metric is BLEU. Avg. time delay is when processing a document image, the ratio of time consumed by layout analysis module to translation module.

Layout Analysis Methods	Translation Quality		Avg. Time Delay
	Regular-layout	Irregular-layout	
Base	35.6	28.9	–
Rule-based	42.9 (+7.3)	37.9 (+9.0)	0.03x
Projection-based	43.4 (+7.8)	38.4 (+9.5)	0.48x
Object Detection-based	43.4 (+7.8)	39.7 (+10.8)	3.5x
Gold-standard Layout	43.6	39.7	–

5   Conclusion

We developed the first document image translation dataset *DITrans* that provides three domains of document images annotated in fine granularity. In addition, benchmark experiments and detailed analysis were conducted on *DITrans* and instructive conclusions on system performance and task difficulties were drawn. With the new task, dataset and framework, we pushed a more comprehensive understanding of document images. In the future, we plan to develop models that are robust to OCR noise and make time-efficient use of the layout structure to promote DIT in both performance and efficiency.

References

1. Antonacopoulos, A., Bridson, D., Papadopoulos, C., Pletschacher, S.: A realistic dataset for performance evaluation of document layout analysis. In: 2009 10th International Conference on Document Analysis and Recognition, pp. 296–300 (2009)
2. Cheng, Y., Tu, Z., Meng, F., Zhai, J., Liu, Y.: Towards robust neural machine translation. In: Proceedings of ACL, pp. 1756–1766 (2018)

3. Guo, H., Qin, X., Liu, J., Han, J., Liu, J., Ding, E.: Eaten: entity-aware attention for single shot visual text extraction. In: 2019 International Conference on Document Analysis and Recognition (ICDAR), pp. 254–259 (2019)
4. Ha, J., Haralick, R.M., Phillips, I.T.: Recursive xy cut using bounding boxes of connected components. In: Proceedings of ICDAR, pp. 952–955 (1995)
5. He, K., Gkioxari, G., Dollár, P., Girshick, R.B.: Mask R-CNN. In: Proceedings of ICCV, pp. 2980–2988 (2017)
6. Jaume, G., Ekenel, H.K., Thiran, J.P.: Funsd: a dataset for form understanding in noisy scanned documents. In: 2019 International Conference on Document Analysis and Recognition Workshops (ICDARW), pp. 1–6 (2019)
7. Jayanthi, S.M., Pruthi, D., Neubig, G.: NeuSpell: a neural spelling correction toolkit. In: Proceedings of EMNLP, pp. 158–164 (2020)
8. Li, M., et al.: DocBank: a benchmark dataset for document layout analysis. In: Proceedings of COLING, pp. 949–960 (2020)
9. Liu, C.L., Yin, F., Wang, D.H., Wang, Q.F.: Casia online and offline chinese handwriting databases. In: Proceedings of ICDAR, pp. 37–41 (2011)
10. Marti, U.V., Bunke, H.: The iam-database: an English sentence database for offline handwriting recognition. Inter. J. Document Anal. Recogn. 39–46 (2002)
11. Park, S., et al.: Cord: a consolidated receipt dataset for post-ocr parsing. In: Workshop on Document Intelligence at NeurIPS 2019 (2019)
12. Rausch, J., Martinez, O., Bissig, F., Zhang, C., Feuerriegel, S.: Docparser: hierarchical document structure parsing from renderings. In: Proceedings of AAAI, pp. 4328–4338 (2021)
13. Ren, S., He, K., Girshick, R.B., Sun, J.: Faster R-CNN: towards real-time object detection with region proposal networks. In: Proceedings of NeurIPS, pp. 91–99 (2015)
14. Vaswani, A., et al.: Attention is all you need. In: Proceedings of NeurIPS, pp. 5998–6008 (2017)
15. Wang, Z., Xu, Y., Cui, L., Shang, J., Wei, F.: LayoutReader: Pre-training of text and layout for reading order detection. In: Proceedings of EMNLP, pp. 4735–4744 (2021)
16. Xu, Y., et al.: Layoutxlm: multimodal pre-training for multilingual visually-rich document understanding. ArXiv (2021)
17. Yu, W., Lu, N., Qi, X., Gong, P., Xiao, R.: Pick: processing key information extraction from documents using improved graph learning-convolutional networks. In: 2020 25th International Conference on Pattern Recognition (ICPR), pp. 4363–4370 (2021)
18. Zhong, X., Tang, J., Jimeno-Yepes, A.: Publaynet: largest dataset ever for document layout analysis. In: 2019 International Conference on Document Analysis and Recognition (ICDAR), pp. 1015–1022 (2019)

Joint Contrastive Learning for Factual Consistency Evaluation of Cross-Lingual Abstract Summarization

Bokai Guo[1,2], Chong Feng[1,2(✉)], Fang Liu[3], Xinyan Li[4], and Xiaomei Wang[5]

[1] School of Computer Science and Technology, Beijing Institute of Technology,
Beijing, China
{bkguo,fengchong}@bit.edu.cn
[2] Southeast Academy of Information Technology, Beijing Institute of Technology,
Beijing, China
[3] School of Foreign Languages, Beijing Institute of Technology, Beijing, China
liufang@bit.edu.cn
[4] China North Vehicle Research Institute, Beijing, China
[5] Institute of Science and Development, Chinese Academy of Sciences, Beijing, China
Wangxm@casisd.cn

Abstract. Current summarization models tend to generate erroneous or irrelevant summaries, i.e., factual inconsistency, which undoubtedly hinders the real-world application of summarization models. The difficulty in language alignment makes factual inconsistency in cross-lingual summarization (CLS) more common and factual consistency checking more challenging. Research on factual consistency has paid little attention to CLS due to the above difficulties, focusing mainly on monolingual summarization (MS). In this paper, we investigate the cross-lingual domain and propose a weakly supervised factual consistency evaluation model for CLS. In particular, we automatically synthesize large-scale datasets by a series of rule-based text transformations and manually annotate the test and validation sets. In addition, we also train the model jointly with contrastive learning to enhance the model's ability to recognize factual errors. The experimental results on the manually annotated test set show that our model can effectively identify the consistency between the summaries and the source documents and outperform the baseline models.

Keywords: Factual consistency evaluation · Cross-lingual summarization · Contrastive learning

1 Introduction

In recent years, natural language generation (NLG) has been fully developed and improved, thanks to Transformer-based [20] pre-trained language models, such as Bert [4] and Bart [13]. Text summarization is an important and challenging subtask of NLG, which can generate a brief summary containing the main

Y. Feng and C. Feng (Eds.): CCMT 2023, CCIS 1922, pp. 116–127, 2023.
https://doi.org/10.1007/978-981-99-7894-6_11

information of the source document [16,18]. The main summarization methods currently include: *extractive* and *abstractive*. Extractive summarization methods select salient sentences from the source document and rearrange them to form the summary, while abstractive summarization methods generate novel sentences by paraphrasing important information in the source document. However, abstract summarization models are unrestricted in their use of words or phrases, leading to the generation of incorrect information (also referred to as hallucinations [17]), which results in factual inconsistency errors. Table 1 shows some factual inconsistency errors generated by CLS models.

Factual consistency means that the information contained in the generated summaries can be fully represented in the source documents. However, previous studies have shown that about 30% of the summaries generated by the state-of-the-art abstract summarization models contain factual inconsistency errors [1,9], which greatly hinders the use of summarization systems in real-world scenarios. The difficulty of aligning different languages makes the evaluation of factual consistency for CLS very challenging. Existing traditional summarization evaluation metrics such as ROUGE [14] and BERTScore [23] lack relevance to factual consistency [17,22]. Additionally, the traditional evaluation metrics require manually annotated reference summaries, which limits the deployment at run-time. Therefore, an automatic evaluation metric for CLS that can be strongly correlated with factual consistency is of practical significance.

Table 1. An example of factual inconsistency errors generated by the CLS model. The factual inconsistency errors in the summary are marked in red, and facts supported by the source document are marked in blue.

En-Zh	Zh-En
Source document: If question marks were raised about whether Aberdeen were about to suffer a serious blow to their aspirations, there seemed no doubt about the validity of Alan Muir's spot-kick award, which Hayes just about squeezed past the Dundee keeper and, from that moment on, the visitors were on the ropes. Dundee's Greg Stewart scores for his side to put them 2-1 up against Aberdeen. Shay Logan's speculative cross was helped on by Shankland and Jack's gamble paid off handsomely as he bundled the ball home from a matter of two yards. Every title-winning team enjoys such moments of relief. (...)	**Source document:** 有人在日本兵库县无人岛海滩发现一个密封透明盒子，里面是一个可水中摄影的数码相机。而且126枚照片都没坏。根据盒里的电子邮箱联系到失主。失主正好是位日本女性，她半年前在菲律宾丢了相机。(*Someone found a sealed transparent box on the beach of No Man Island in Hyogo Prefecture, Japan, containing a digital camera that can be used for underwater photography. And none of the 126 photos are damaged. Contact the owner according to the email in the box. The owner happened to be a Japanese woman who lost her camera in the Philippines six months ago.*)
Summary: 阿伯丁周六在苏格兰足球超级联赛以2比1击败邓迪。(*Aberdeen beat Dundee 2-1 in the Scottish Football Super League on Saturday.*)	**Summary:** 126 cameras lost on the beach of no man's island, japan.

In this paper, we focus on cross-lingual abstract summarization and propose a weakly supervised automatic evaluation metric for factual consistency. At the same time, due to the lack of cross-lingual datasets for factual consistency evaluation, we construct large-scale English-Chinese (En-Zh) and Chinese-English (Zh-En) datasets[1], where the training set is automatically synthesized, and test and validation sets are formed by manually annotating the outputs of the CLS model. In general, for source documents D, consistency summary S^+ and inconsistency summary S^-, D and S^+ should be closer in the embedding space than D and S^-, since S^+ conforms to D and S^- departs from D. Therefore, we introduce contrastive learning to enable the model to better distinguish between consistent and inconsistent summaries. The experimental results show that we provide a reliable and effective automatic evaluation method that can be applied to factual consistency checking for CLS.

2   Related Work

Previous work on factual consistency metrics can be classified into two categories: unsupervised and weakly supervised [10]. Unsupervised metrics leverage existing models from other tasks to indirectly evaluate factual consistency without additional supervised data, while weakly supervised metrics use automatically synthesized data to train a new classification model to evaluate factual consistency.

For unsupervised metrics, Goodrich et al. [9] propose to utilize fact triples (*subject, relation, object*) to evaluate factual consistency. The author constructed a new fact extraction dataset on Wikipedia articles and trained a Transformer-based model to extract the fact triples of source documents and summaries respectively, and then checked factual consistency based on the overlap of these triples. Falke et al. [7] resort to natural language inference (NLI) models to detect factual errors under the assumption that a faithful summary should be fully entailed by the source document. Laban et al. [12] refine the NLI dataset by partitioning the document into multiple sentences and then aggregating the scores between these sentences and the summary, achieving a good improvement. Wang et al. [21] and Durmus et al. [5] use a question answering (QA) model to judge whether the summaries and the source document are factually consistent. This method allows the summary and the source document to answer the same question separately, and then evaluate factual consistency based on the similarity of their answers. Fabbri et al. [6] propose to combine textual entailment and QA models to further improve the performance. The above metrics all rely on existing models from other tasks to check factual consistency, but they do not overcome the domain differences between these other tasks and text summarization.

For weakly supervised metrics, the datasets are heuristically generated rather than manually annotated, considerably reducing the enormous cost of manual annotation. Kryscinski et al. [11] inspired by the error analysis of state-of-the-art

---

[1] The dataset is available on this link: https://github.com/anonymousdataset/dataset-CLS.

summarization model outputs, automatically synthesize the dataset by a series of text transformations on the CNN/DM [18] dataset and propose the sentence-level factual consistency checking model called FactCC. Zhou et al. [25] propose a more fine-grained token-level metric on the XSUM [19] dataset, which can identify factually inconsistent tokens in summaries. Zhao et al. [24] propose a new method, HERMAN, for detecting quantity errors (e.g., numbers, sum of money, dates, etc.) in summaries. All of above methods achieve good improvements, but still focus only on the monolingual summarization.

3   Approach

In this section, we present the construction method of the factual consistency evaluation dataset for CLS, and the training method of joint contrastive learning.

3.1   Synthetic Training Set

The training set in this work is automatically synthesized for two key reasons: (1) cross-lingual parallel corpora for factual consistency evaluation are scarce and manual annotation of datasets is prohibitively expensive and time-consuming; (2) previous work has shown that outputs of the abstract summarization models contain errors typically related to named entities, numbers, and pronouns. Therefore, inspired by the text transformations proposed by Kryscinski et al. [11], we finally created large-scale weakly supervised En-Zh and Zh-En training sets.

Text Transformations. In this work, five types of transformations were performed: *Round-trip Translation, Entity* swapping, *Number* swapping, *Pronoun* swapping, and *Sentence Negation*. For a source document D_A in language A, S_B is the reference summary in different language B. As shown in Table 2, we perform text transformations for the reference summary S_B. Specifically, for *Round-trip Translation*, we use the Google Translate[2] to first translate S_B into pivot languages, including English, German, French, and Chinese, and then back into the original language. For *Entity* and *Number* swapping[3], an entity in the reference summary S_B is randomly replaced by a different entity of the same type in the source document. Since the source language and the target language are different, we also use Google Translate to translate the entities in the source document to the corresponding target language before swapping them. For *Pronoun* swapping and *Sentence Negation*, we replace the pronouns and negation words in the summaries randomly with the opposite words respectively. The original reference summaries and the summaries generated by *Round-trip Translation* are labeled as positive (*consistent*). The summaries generated by the rest of the text transformations are labeled as negative (*inconsistent*). Since the outputs

---

[2] https://translate.google.com.
[3] In this work, the spaCy's NER model extracts all entities. https://spacy.io.

of the neural CLS model contain certain noise, we randomly perturb the training data to enhance the robustness by randomly duplicating or deleting each token of the summaries with a certain probability. We finally created the training set $D_{train} = (D_A, S_B^+, S_B^-)$. S_B^+ and S_B^- denote consistent summaries and inconsistent summaries, respectively.

Table 2. An example of text transformations to create pseudo summaries.

Source document: A 19-year-old who brutally beat up a 70-year-old man in Portland, Oregon while high on drugs refused to apologize to the victim today as he was sentenced to five years in prison. Daniel Dorson, then 18, smashed his skateboard over Larry Allen's head when the senior citizen asked him and a group of street youth to move away from the Portland Outdoor Store, where he has worked for the past 30 years. Public defender Chris Howard made a deal with prosecutor Chris Mascal, agreeing that if Dorson plead guilty to attempted second-degree assault, he would get a five-year sentence with the possibility of early release. (...)

Reference summary: 多森被判5年监禁，但由于认罪协议，他可能提前获释。 (*Dorson was sentenced to five years, but due to a plea agreement, he may be released early.*)

Round-trip Translation: 多森被判处5年徒刑，但他通过认罪协议可能提前释放。 (*Dotson was sentenced to five years in prison, but he may be released early through a plea agreement.*)

Entity swap: 拉里·艾伦被判5年监禁，但由于认罪协议，他可能提前获释。 (*Larry Allen was sentenced to five years, but due to a plea agreement, he may be released early.*)

Number swap: 多森被判30年监禁，但由于认罪协议，他可能提前获释。 (*Dorson was sentenced to 30 years, but due to a plea agreement, he may be released early.*)

Pronoun swap: 多森被判5年监禁，但由于认罪协议，她可能提前获释。 (*Dorson was sentenced to five years, but due to a plea agreement, she may be released early.*)

Sentence negation: 多森被判5年监禁，但由于认罪协议，他不可能提前获释。 (*Dorson was sentenced to five years, but due to a plea agreement, he can't be released early.*)

3.2 Human-Annotated Test/Validation Set

In contrast to the automatically synthesized training set, we manually annotated the test and validation set. To obtain the data to be labeled, we fine-tuned mBART [15] on the NCLS[4] dataset [26], and then manually labeled the outputs of mBART. The annotators are proficient in both English and Chinese. It is worth noting that we ignore the unreadable summaries generated by mBART because they do not make sense.

3.3 Model

A summary is consistent if it is completely supported by the source document, otherwise it is inconsistent. So the evaluation model is essentially a binary classification model. Further, we jointly train this classification model with contrastive

---

[4] NCLS is the En-Zh and Zh-En cross-lingual summarization dataset.

learning to aggregate the representations of source documents with consistent summaries and to push out the representations with inconsistent summaries. As shown in Fig. 1, the model jointly trains with classification and contrastive learning.

Classification Training. XLM-Roberta [2] is a transformer-based multilingual masked language model, pre-trained on 100 languages, with superior performance on natural language understanding (NLU) tasks such as cross-lingual classification, sequence labeling, and question answering. Therefore, we choose the XLM-Roberta as the base model and fine-tune it on the synthetic dataset. Specifically, we concatenate consistent summaries S_B^+ or inconsistent summaries S_B^- with D_A in the training set D_{train} as the inputs, and then the model predicts the labels with positive (*consistent*) or negative (*inconsistent*). The classification loss L_{CE} uses the standard cross-entropy loss function as follows:

$$L_{CE} = -\frac{1}{N}\sum_i [y_i \cdot log(p_i) + (1 - y_i) \cdot log(1 - p_i)] \tag{1}$$

where N denotes the number of samples in a mini-batch; y_i is the true label of sample i with a value of 0 or 1; and P_i denotes the probability of predicting the true category.

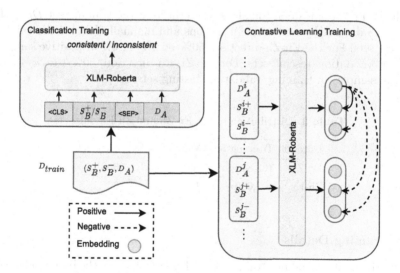

Fig. 1. The main training process of the model.

Contrastive Learning Training. Contrastive learning aims to learn embedding representations by pulling positive samples together and pushing negative samples away. As shown in Fig. 1, for the i-th data $(D_A^i, S_B^{i+}, S_B^{i-})$ in training set D_{train}, the summary S_B^{i+} is consistent with the source document D_A^i, so we can treat D_A^i and S_B^{i+} as positive samples for each other, while the inconsistent summary S_B^{i-} as negative samples. In addition, inspired by supervised SimCSE [8], we also take the remaining samples in the same batch as negative samples, and the contrastive learning loss function L_{CL} is as follows:

$$L_{CL} = -\log \frac{e^{sim(z_i,z_i^+)/\tau}}{\sum_{j=1}^{N} \left(e^{sim(z_i,z_j^+)/\tau} + e^{sim(z_i,z_j^-)/\tau} \right)} \tag{2}$$

where N denotes the number of samples in a mini-batch; z_i, z_i^+, z_j^- denote the representations of source documents D_A, consistent summaries S_B^+, and inconsistent summaries S_B^- , respectively; τ denotes a temperature hyperparameter; and $sim(z_i, z_j) = \frac{z_i^\top z_j}{\|z_i\| \cdot \|z_j\|}$ denotes cosine similarity.

Formally, the final loss functions L is joint classification loss L_{CE} and contrastive learning loss L_{CL} as follows:

$$L = L_{CE} + L_{CL} \tag{3}$$

4　Experiments

4.1　Datasets

As shown in Table 3, we automatically synthesized the training set D_{train} from the NCLS dataset by text transformations and manually labeled the validation and test sets. For the En-Zh direction, 50%/66.5%/71.3% of positive samples in training/validation/testing sets; For the Zh-En direction, 50%/61.4%/72.6% of positive samples in training/validation/testing sets.

Table 3. Distribution of the En-Zh and Zh-En datasets

Dataset	Training Set	Validation Set	Test Set
En-Zh	163,810	400	350
Zh-En	407,080	400	300

4.2　Training Details

We use the multilingual pre-trained XLM-Roberta-base as the base model, which has 12 hidden layers and 12 attention heads per layer. For the En-Zh and Zh-En, the model is both trained with 3 epochs on the dataset D_{train}. The maximum length of inputs in the En-Zh and Zh-En directions are both 512. The learning rate is set to 2e−5, and the weight decay is 0.01. The temperature hyperparameter τ is set to 0.05. To speed up the model training, we use the half-precision floating-point format (FP16), which allows the model to be present on the GPU in 16-bit precision.

4.3   Baselines

We compared the following baselines with our model:

XLM-Roberta+XNLI. XNLI [3] is a cross-lingual natural language inference corpus supporting 15 languages. The natural language inference task is to determine whether the semantic logical relationship between two sentences is *entailment, contradiction,* or *neutral,* which is similar to the goal of factual consistency checking. Therefore, the XLM-Roberta-large fine-tuned on the XNLI is used as the baseline, and we throw away the *neutral* label.

FactCC. Kryscinski et al. [11] proposed this model for factual consistency checking of monolingual summarization. The authors also proposed the FactCCX model, which adds span selection heads to the FactCC. The span selection heads allow the model to highlight interdependent spans of the source document and the summary.

SummaC-Conv. Laban et al. [12] proposed this trained model, consisting of a learned convolutional layer that aggregates the entailment scores for all document sentences into a single score. Specifically, for a source document of M sentences and a summary of N sentences, a NLI model is first utilized to generate an $M \times N$ score matrix, and then the columns of the matrix are binned to generate an $H \times N$ bin matrix, which is then passed through a $1 - D$ convolutional layer. Finally the scores of each summary sentence are averaged to form an overall score.

5   Results and Analysis

5.1   Main Results

We compare the performance of our model with baselines on the manually annotated test sets described in Sect. 3.2, and show the experimental results in Table 4, illustrating the significant improvement achieved by our approach over the baselines.

On the En-Zh test set, our model improves about 2.32 in accuracy and about 0.92 in macro F1-score compared to baselines. On the Zh-En test set, our model achieves an even higher improvement, with accuracy and macro F1-score improving by about 9.57 and 7.74, respectively. It is worth noting that our model show significant performance improvement on the Zh-En test set compared to the En-Zh test set, possibly due to the difference in data length. The average document lengths on the En-Zh and Zh-En training sets are 711 and 80, respectively, which makes the model easier to train in the Zh-En direction. Meanwhile, the maximum token length of our model is 512, resulting in the possible loss of critical information in the En-Zh direction. These explain the better performance of our model in the Zh-En test set.

Table 4. The experimental results in the En-Zh and Zh-En manually annotated test sets. Macro F1($\times 100$) is the macro-average of the F1 between the two classes. The $+CL$ denotes joint contrastive learning to train our model. The $*$ means that the Chinese texts in the test set was translated into English for evaluation.

Models	En-Zh		Zh-En	
	Accuracy	Macro F1	Accuracy	Macro F1
XLM-R+XNLI	60.69	51.60	68.52	59.00
FactCC*	65.89	62.36	53.13	52.07
FactCCX*	65.31	61.09	59.73	56.11
SummaC-Conv*	73.98	55.22	71.61	65.09
Ours+CL	**76.30**	**63.28**	**81.18**	**72.83**

5.2 Ablation Study

To demonstrate the effectiveness of our proposed approach, we carried out the ablation experiment as shown in Table 5. The experimental results show that our model trained without contrastive learning suffers from performance degradation. On the En-Zh and Zh-En test sets, the results of the model trained with contrastive learning improved by 2.32 and 3.30 in accuracy, and improved by 0.87 and 5.83 in macro F1-score, respectively. Experimental results demonstrate that joint contrastive learning training improves the model's ability to distinguish factual consistency between source documents and summaries.

Table 5. Experimental results of the ablation study. $+CL$ and $-CL$ denotes that training our model with and without contrastive learning, respectively.

Models	En-Zh		Zh-En	
	Accuracy	Macro F1	Accuracy	Macro F1
Ours-CL	73.98	62.41	77.88	67.00
Ours+CL	**76.30**	**63.28**	**81.18**	**72.83**

5.3 Analysis of Contrastive Learning Effectiveness

We jointly contrastive learning to train the model to pull together representations between source documents and consistent summaries, while pushing away representations with inconsistent summaries. To confirm this conclusion, we compute the embedding vector distances to the source documents for the consistency summaries and inconsistency summaries separately. Specifically, we randomly select 50 each of the consistent and inconsistent summaries in the test set and compute the average cosine similarity distance to the source documents. As shown in Fig. 2, it demonstrates that models trained by joint contrastive learning indeed push apart the representations between positive and negative samples. It is worth noting that the cosine similarity distance is around 0.7 even for the negative samples, owing to the fact that errors in the inconsistent summaries may occur only for a several words such as entity, date, etc., and thus the sentence representations of the inconsistent summaries and the source documents are somehow near each other.

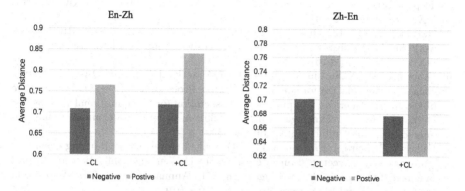

Fig. 2. Positive or Negative denotes the cosine similarity distances of the consistent or inconsistent summaries from the source documents; CL denotes contrastive learning.

6 Conclusion

In this paper, to measure the factual consistency of CLS, we propose an evaluation model. Simultaneously, we train the model jointly with contrastive learning to bring the representations closer between the consistent summaries and source documents. In addition, we automatically synthesize large-scale En-Zh and Zh-En datasets using text transformations and manually annotate the test and validation sets. The experimental results show that our model achieves excellent performance on the manually annotated test set and outperforms previous models. Overall, our approach can be applied to automatic metrics of factual consistency, responding to the credibility of CLS systems.

The limitation of our model is the ineffectiveness of distinguishing commonsense errors, so in future work we would like to focus on identifying such errors. In addition, we also investigate on factual consistency evaluation for other NLG tasks, such as machine translation.

Acknowledgements. This work is supported by the Institute of Science and Development, Chinese Academy of Sciences (GHJ-ZLZX-2023-04). We would like to thank the anonymous reviewers for their thoughtful and constructive comments.

References

1. Cao, Z., Wei, F., Li, W., Li, S.: Faithful to the original: fact aware neural abstractive summarization. In: Proceedings of the AAAI Conference on Artificial Intelligence, vol. 32 (2018)

2. Conneau, A., et al.: Unsupervised cross-lingual representation learning at scale. arXiv preprint arXiv:1911.02116 (2019)
3. Conneau, A., et al.: XNLI: evaluating cross-lingual sentence representations. In: Proceedings of the 2018 Conference on Empirical Methods in Natural Language Processing. Association for Computational Linguistics (2018)
4. Devlin, J., Chang, M.W., Lee, K., Toutanova, K.: BERT: pre-training of deep bidirectional transformers for language understanding. arXiv preprint arXiv:1810.04805 (2018)
5. Durmus, E., He, H., Diab, M.: FEQA: a question answering evaluation framework for faithfulness assessment in abstractive summarization. arXiv preprint arXiv:2005.03754 (2020)
6. Fabbri, A., Wu, C.S., Liu, W., Xiong, C.: QAFactEval: improved QA-based factual consistency evaluation for summarization. In: Proceedings of the 2022 Conference of the North American Chapter of the Association for Computational Linguistics: Human Language Technologies, pp. 2587–2601. Association for Computational Linguistics, Seattle, United States, July 2022
7. Falke, T., Ribeiro, L.F., Utama, P.A., Dagan, I., Gurevych, I.: Ranking generated summaries by correctness: an interesting but challenging application for natural language inference. In: Proceedings of the 57th Annual Meeting of the Association for Computational Linguistics, pp. 2214–2220 (2019)
8. Gao, T., Yao, X., Chen, D.: SimCSE: simple contrastive learning of sentence embeddings. arXiv preprint arXiv:2104.08821 (2021)
9. Goodrich, B., Rao, V., Liu, P.J., Saleh, M.: Assessing the factual accuracy of generated text. In: Proceedings of the 25th ACM SIGKDD International Conference on Knowledge Discovery and Data Mining, pp. 166–175 (2019)
10. Huang, Y., Feng, X., Feng, X., Qin, B.: The factual inconsistency problem in abstractive text summarization: a survey. arXiv preprint arXiv:2104.14839 (2021)
11. Kryściński, W., McCann, B., Xiong, C., Socher, R.: Evaluating the factual consistency of abstractive text summarization. arXiv preprint arXiv:1910.12840 (2019)
12. Laban, P., Schnabel, T., Bennett, P.N., Hearst, M.A.: Summac: re-visiting NLI-based models for inconsistency detection in summarization. Trans. Assoc. Comput. Linguist. **10**, 163–177 (2022)
13. Lewis, M., et al.: BART: denoising sequence-to-sequence pre-training for natural language generation, translation, and comprehension. arXiv preprint arXiv:1910.13461 (2019)
14. Lin, C.Y.: Rouge: a package for automatic evaluation of summaries. In: Text Summarization Branches Out, pp. 74–81 (2004)
15. Liu, Y., et al.: Multilingual denoising pre-training for neural machine translation. Trans. Assoc. Comput. Linguist. **8**, 726–742 (2020)
16. Mani, I., Maybury, M.T.: Advances in Automatic Text Summarization. MIT Press, Cambridge (1999)
17. Maynez, J., Narayan, S., Bohnet, B., McDonald, R.: On faithfulness and factuality in abstractive summarization. arXiv preprint arXiv:2005.00661 (2020)
18. Nallapati, R., Zhou, B., Gulcehre, C., Xiang, B., et al.: Abstractive text summarization using sequence-to-sequence RNNs and beyond. arXiv preprint arXiv:1602.06023 (2016)
19. Narayan, S., Cohen, S.B., Lapata, M.: Don't give me the details, just the summary! Topic-aware convolutional neural networks for extreme summarization. arXiv preprint arXiv:1808.08745 (2018)
20. Vaswani, A., et al.: Attention is all you need. In: Advances in Neural Information Processing Systems, vol. 30 (2017)

21. Wang, A., Cho, K., Lewis, M.: Asking and answering questions to evaluate the factual consistency of summaries. arXiv preprint arXiv:2004.04228 (2020)
22. Wang, C., Sennrich, R.: On exposure bias, hallucination and domain shift in neural machine translation. In: Proceedings of the 58th Annual Meeting of the Association for Computational Linguistics, pp. 3544–3552. Association for Computational Linguistics, July 2020
23. Zhang, T., Kishore, V., Wu, F., Weinberger, K.Q., Artzi, Y.: BERTscore: evaluating text generation with BERT. arXiv preprint arXiv:1904.09675 (2019)
24. Zhao, Z., Cohen, S.B., Webber, B.: Reducing quantity hallucinations in abstractive summarization. arXiv preprint arXiv:2009.13312 (2020)
25. Zhou, C., et al.: Detecting hallucinated content in conditional neural sequence generation. arXiv preprint arXiv:2011.02593 (2020)
26. Zhu, J., et al.: NCLs: neural cross-lingual summarization. arXiv preprint arXiv:1909.00156 (2019)

Author Index

Printed in the United States
by Baker & Taylor Publisher Services